D0983869

THE GODOLPHIN ARABIAN
The Story of the Matchem Line

MORDAUNT MILNER

THE
GODOLPHIN
ARABIAN
The Story of the Matchem Line

J. A. ALLEN · LONDON

To my wife

First published in Great Britain by
J. A. Allen & Co Ltd
1 Lower Grosvenor Place
Buckingham Palace Road
London SW1W 0EL
1990

British Library Cataloguing in Publication Data
Milner, Mordaunt
   The Godolphin Arabian: the story of the Matchem
line.
   1. Racehorses, history
   I. Title
   636.1′2′09

   ISBN 0–85131–476–7

Phototypeset in 11/13 point Ehrhardt
by Input Typesetting Ltd, London SW19 8DR
Printed and bound by
Billings & Sons Ltd, Worcester

CONTENTS

LIST OF ILLUSTRATIONS

Page 7
Marcovil's son, Hurry On.
Hurry On's second Derby winner, Coronach.

Page 8
Montrose, one of Coronach's sons.
Relic, the son of War Relic who revitalised the Matchem line in
    Europe just after the Second World War.

PREFACE

I have used the descendants of the Godolphin Arabian, known as the Matchem line, merely as a path to follow the story of the Turf through twenty or so generations. No claim is made that this male line is superior to that of the Darley Arabian or that of the Byerley Turk. None of them succeeded in passing on their male line through more than one source, which makes it a triple dead-heat as far as the original Eastern horses are concerned.

CHAPTER 1

THE GODOLPHIN ARABIAN, THE MATCHEM LINE

His proud neck arched, his bold eyes flashing and his nostrils flaring, an Arab stallion walks with prancing gait. He is bridled and reined with silken cords; tassels hang from his breastplate and saddle. His rider sits on him somewhat nonchalantly, trusting his fiery steed to the firm hold of two attendants, clad in the livery of jockeys of the eighteenth century, for the ground that he is pawing is not the hot sand of Arabia but the green turf of the Knavesmire or Newmarket. The rider, both by his dress and his demeanour, is evidently a stranger to these parts for he holds out a pointing finger, apparently asking the way to the starting post, where three horses can be seen waiting in the background. Edgar Wallace wrote a short story about a small boy, dangerously ill, who wished to see before he died what he described as a 'proud horse'. The horse depicted would have been just what the doctor ordered. The proud horse is Sham, the Godolphin Arabian.

The picture, Turner's frontispiece to Eugene Sue's fantasy about the Godolphin Arabian, may be as highly imaginative as the book itself and may depict a casting director's notion of the ideal Arab, but it may also be a good likeness according to those who saw Sham in life.

Sham, the name if pronounced to rhyme with 'charm' not 'ham', was a dark bay brown with a white mark on the inside of his off hind coronet. He was a horse of great beauty with a wild haughty appearance. He had the head of the typical Arabian, full of fire and character, though more masculine than pretty, which is probably why one writer describes a certain plainness of head and ears.

His head was set on a beautifully curved neck with a pronounced crest, 'the Knight of the Wonderful Crest' Nimrod called him. He was a short-backed horse with muscled loins and a high, broad croup. The muscles of his loins were 'inserted into his quarters with greater strength and power than in any horse yet seen of his dimensions'. He stood 14.2 hh. One critic states that he was narrow in front and rather on the leg, but the Vicomte de Manty, who saw Sham when he was in France, writes,

'He was of beautiful conformation, exquisitely proportioned with large hocks, well let down, with legs of iron, with unequalled lightness of forehand – a horse of incomparable beauty whose only flaw was being headstrong. An essentially strong stallion type, his quarters broad in spite of being half starved, tail carried in true Arabian style.'

What one writer describes as 'narrow in front' appears to another as 'unequalled lightness of forehand'. In any case to be narrow in front might well have been a virtue, for of all the breeds of horses the Thoroughbred is the narrowest in front and a stallion of this type would have helped to mould the breed in the early days of Thoroughbred evolution.

Sham was foaled in the dark ages before Volume One of the General Stud Book had been published and of all the horses of that era of myth and legend none has been the subject of more fantasies than Sham. Lady Wentworth, by far the most reliable source, has carefully presented all the evidence, factual, written and hearsay, as to the origins of this Arabian. It seems that he was of the Jilfan blood of Yemen, and was exported via Syria to the stud of the Bey of Tunis. In 1730 the Bey presented four Arabian horses to the King of France. Three of these were turned out in the forests of Brittany to improve the local stock and the other, who was Sham, was sold to Edward Coke, the proprietor of St James's Coffee House, for his stud at Longford Hall in Derbyshire.

One of the myths concerning Sham tells of the Arabian pulling a water cart during his stay in France, a story often repeated in print. It appeared in Professor Ridgeway's treatise on the origins of the Thoroughbred, and Theo Taunton in *Famous Horses* writes

that the Godolphin was believed to have been stolen and subsequently bought from the owner of a water cart. This is nonsense
but every legend springs from a well of truth, however distorted
it may become in the re-telling. The Vicomte, whose words were
quoted previously, writes,

'The horses arrived in poor condition and were very thin,
and, though put in the Royal stables, were despised and
neglected and the grooms disliked them because they were
quick and fiery and hard to ride. One of these was Shami, a
bay brown with reddish mottle and very little white on his
hind feet.'

Here, then, is the origin of the tale. It would be a small step from
saying 'in poor condition' to 'half-starved' to 'looks has if he has
been pulling a cart'. The description of his temperament destroys
the truth of the story as effectively as Sham would have broken
up the cart.

In 1733 Mr Coke died and bequeathed his mares to the second
Earl of Godolphin, who then bought Sham from Roger Williams,
who had inherited the stallions of the stud. And so Sham became
the Godolphin Arabian, and remained so for at least a hundred
years, as it was then that Nimrod, the best-known Turf historian
of the period, wrote, 'In his reign [viz. George II's] the Godolphin
Arabian appeared, the founder of our best blood.' Then suddenly,
with as little evidence as there is to attribute the works of Shake-
speare to Bacon or Marlowe or Lord Tom Noddy, some writers
decided that the Godolphin Arabian was a Barb. This conclusion
was reached on two premises – portraits of Sham and the 'failure'
of the Godolphin line.

The chief 'barbarian' was a Captain Upton who wrote,

'The original portrait of the Godolphin Arabian I have not
seen. All the prints of him do not correspond; but the impres-
sion of the countenance and the outline of the head as generally depicted would lead me to the supposition that he was a
horse of Northern Africa (commonly called a Barb) and not
of pure or unmixed blood, which can be further strengthened

by the drawing of the ears, which are shown as lopping outwards.'

The gallant captain was right to say that all the prints do not correspond. Most of them do not even show the correct markings and are not even of the horse. However, the compilers of the General Stud Book took Captain Upton's venture in art criticism seriously and inserted the following in the Stud Book:

'Whether he was an Arabian or a Barb is a point disputed (his portrait would rather lead to the latter supposition) but his excellence as a stallion is generally admitted. There is an original portrait of the horse in Lord Cholmondely's collection at Houghton. Comparing it with Mr Stubbs' print of him, it will seem that disproportionately small limbs as represented in the latter do not accord with the painting.'

Another to have been misled by this picture more recently was Martin E. Eversfield, contributor to *Thoroughbred Breeding of the World*, published in Germany in 1970. He writes,

'this brown Barb standing about fifteen hands (looking at his picture we are tempted to accept the fact of his Moroccan origin) was so prepotent in his stud career that he rivalled for the leadership with the other two "legs of the tripod", the Byerley Turk and the Darley Arabian. . . . Students of the effect left on the Thoroughbred by both Arabian and Barb believe that the "Godolphin" was possessed of a lesser degree of prepotency because he was not a horse of pure Arabian origin, the latter being credited with more outstanding prepotency.'

This is an extraordinary surmise. Does the writer suggest that the Alcock Arabian, Gibson's Grey Arabian, the Honeywood White Arabian, the Malcolm Arabian, the Bloody Shouldered Arabian, Bell's Arabian, the Woodstock Arabian, the Lonsdale Bay Arabian, Oglethorpe's Arabian, the Oysterfoot Arabian, the Cyprus Arabian, Litton's Chestnut Arabian *et al* could not have been Arabians because they possessed 'a lesser degree of potency' than did Sham if Sham was a Barb?

The portrait at Houghton is not an original but a copy of what is alleged to have been an original painting by David Morier. The Houghton painting was not painted from life and it seems it might have been painted many years after Sham's death because it bears the inscription:

'Esteemed one of the best Foreign Horses ever brought to England. Appearing so both from the country he came from and from the Performance of his Posterity. They being Excellent both as Racers and Stallions and Hitting with most other Pedigrees and mending ye Imperfections of Their Shape. And is allowed to have refreshed the English Blood more than any Foreign Horse ever imported.'

Whoever worded the inscription begged the question of the horse's breed and origin. He must have been puzzled, for the horse depicted was undoubtedly a Barb, while at that time there was no suggestion that Sham was anything but an Arabian.

Now Lord Godolphin had a Barb, in fact he had two Barbs. One was a grey and the other was a brown, the same colour as Sham except that he had a star. It seems possible that David Morier, asked to paint the Godolphin Arabian when he had become so famous after his death, may have used Lord Godolphin's Brown Western Barb as a model, painting in Sham's markings and his famous crest.

There is a portrait of the Godolphin Arabian painted by Wootton, signed by the artist and dated 1731. The horse is undoubtedly Arabian and is undoubtedly Sham.

C. M. Prior, who wrote so many books on the early history of the Thoroughbred and who had in his possession the manuscript stud books of both Edward Coke and Lord Godolphin, wrote,

'In case any doubt should still exist after the written testimony of both his owners and anyone should persist in saying that the Godolphin was a Barb, the evidence of Osmer should be conclusive on this point. He knew the horse better than any other writer, as he was personally well acquainted with him, and invariably alluded to him as an Arabian, further mentioning that "Barbs may in general easily be known by an observant eye".'

The suggestion of the 'failure' of the Godolphin line might similarly be said of St Simon, since both stallions dominated the breed of the Thoroughbred in their time. The impact of the Godolphin Arabian on the breed is amazing considering how sparingly he was used: he sired only ninety foals in a stud career of twenty-two years. The veterinary surgeon, Osmer, mentioned above, writing shortly after Sham's death says, 'It was a pity that he was not used more universally for better mares.' Despite this, the Stud Book (1858) states: 'It is remarkable that there is not a superior horse now on the Turf without a cross of the Godolphin Arabian, neither has there been for many years past.'

The Godolphin arrived at stud a generation or so later than many of the other great Eastern horses. Gossip about him started right away. It was said that he was used as a teaser for Hobgoblin, and that it was only after the latter refused to cover Roxana that Sham was used. Lady Wentworth has given her version of Eugene Sue's description of the mating from his extravaganza, which is worth repeating for her footnote. 'We have the melodramatic story of his fight with Hobgoblin for the lovely Roxana; the horses trying to stun each other with furious charges forehead to forehead.' Lady Wentworth's delightfully malicious comment is: 'Sue's fostermother as a child was a nanny goat, which perhaps explains his primitive ideas of fighting by butting.' C. M. Prior discounts the whole story on the grounds that, firstly since Hobgoblin was racing in 1730 and 1732, it is unlikely that he would have been brought back to stud in 1731, and secondly there is no record in Lord Godolphin's stud book that Hobgoblin covered any mares in 1735. On the other hand the reverse might be true, i.e. that he went to stud in 1731 and, because of his failure to do his duty, was brought back to racing in 1732. Whether the story is true or not is immaterial. The Godolphin Arabian was mated with Roxana and the result was the good racehorse, Lath.

Lath was the best racehorse of his day. He beat Squirt, who was to become the grandsire of Eclipse, in the Great Stakes at Newmarket. Although there is no record of the distance over which this race was run, all the runners carried the same weight of 8 stone 7 lbs and they were all of the same age so it might be said to have been a forerunner of the classics as we know them today although this race was for four-year-olds. It was not until 1858 that the ages of racehorses were reckoned from New Year's Day and in the old days, much more sensibly and more naturally, their official birthday was the first of May; it was a mistake to have changed it. As the Great Stakes (a splendid name – I wonder why it is not used today?) was run at the end of April, the classic contenders were almost five-year-olds.

A son of the Godolphin Arabian with not such a splendid name was Cripple, but Cripple's son had a name that is almost as well known today as that of Matchem. This was the little dark grey horse, Gimcrack – 'the sweetest little horse that ever was,' as Lady Sarah Bunbury declared when she saw Gimcrack win. 'And the sweetest little horse he has remained to every lover of the Turf from that day to this,' as Sir Thomas Cook has added. This great stayer raced for eight seasons and won twenty-five races all over the country, but oddly he was beaten the only two times he ran at York, where the race bearing his name is run and where the owner of the winner is allowed a free rein at the Gimcrack Dinner to tell the guests how racing should be run. Gimcrack must have been one of the first racehorses to have crossed to France, as his wins over long distances prompted Count Lauraguais to buy him to win a bet that a horse could cover 22½ miles in an hour; the Count won his bet and Gimcrack returned to England to continue his winning ways. As he only stood about 14 hh he was always a good thing in give and take races, which were handicapped by height so he made a speciality of them.

Another of the progeny of the Godolphin is commemorated by a race to this day – the Selima Stakes for two-year-old fillies at Laurel. Selima was exported to the States in 1750 and was unbeaten there. In addition to the stake money for the Selima Stakes there is a cup bearing the inscription: 'This cup is presented by Belair Stud (William Woodward, owner) in memory of Selima (by the Godolphin Arabian) imported to Belair in the reign of George the Second, Selima the ancestress of Hanover, Foxhall and many fine racehorses.'

Regulus, whom Sham got in 1739, won seven Royal Plates and was never beaten. He is a most important link in the chain of Thoroughbred inheritance as he is the sire of Spiletta, the dam of Eclipse. it is recorded in the General Stud Book that 'Eclipse was so called, not because he eclipsed all his competitors, but from having been foaled during the great eclipse in 1764.' He was bred by the Duke of Cumberland, who did not live to see what a great horse his famous stud had produced, and was sold to a Mr Wildman when little more than a yearling. Wildman turned up late for the sale but found it had started too early so, with his eye on Eclipse, insisted that the lots be resold. He did not race the colt until he was five. Eclipse won his first heat and it was after that Dennis O'Kelly made his famous bet of 'Eclipse first and the rest nowhere'. His bet came off as, in the second heat, Eclipse outdistanced the others, a distance being 240 yards. O'Kelly bought a half-share in the horse, who throughout his career showed himself to be head and shoulders above any other Thoroughbred. Eclipse won every race he contested with astonishing ease, he was sound in wind and limb, and could carry big weights; in addition to his speed and stride he could stay, and was never thoroughly tested.

Another daughter of Regulus was the dam of MacHeath, who in seven weeks travelled and raced 500 miles winning six four-year-old plates. One of the first Thoroughbreds to make a name for himself in the United States was Brutus, a roan son of Regulus and Miss Layton. Miss Layton, also known as Lodge's Roan Mare, was descended from a Barb mare given by the Emperor of Morocco to Lord Arlington when he was Secretary of State for King Charles II. Edward Fenwick, a relation of the breeder of Matchem, had established a large stud in South Carolina and imported a number of stallions and mares from England. Naturally, in view of his family's successes with the son of Cade, he was very keen on the blood of the Godolphin Arabian. Brutus was most successful there.

Babraham, another son of the Godolphin, was far more typical physically of the line as we have known it in this century than the little grey Gimcrack. He was 'a fine, strong horse, 16 hands high and master of 18 stone'. So near to the original Arab source this was an exceptional height and he is the only horse whose height comes in for specific mention in the General Stud Book. He won numerous races in 1748 and managed to cover fifty-three mares in the same season. He met defeat at the hands of another son of the Godolphin, Bajazet, over six miles at Newmarket, each carrying 12 stone.

The Godolphin bred another successful sire, particularly of broodmares, in Blank. The phenomenal success of the Duke of Grafton's stud owed a lot to Blank's daughter, Julia. Mated to a daughter of Regulus he bred Rachel. This mare, who was inbred to the Godolphin Arabian with no free generations (2 x 2), bred the unbeaten Highflyer, who was born beneath the Highflyer walnut trees in the paddocks of Sir Charles Bunbury, who won the first Derby with Diomed. He was buried at Highflyer Hall, built near Ely by Mr Tattersall, where the memorial stone reads:

'Here lieth the perfect and beautiful symmetry of the much lamented Highflyer, by whom and his wonderful offspring the celebrated Tattersall acquired a noble fortune, but was not ashamed to acknowledge it.'

Highflyer was not named immediately, which was unfortunate and would have saved a deal of argument as Highflyer's unbeaten record depends on the records of two races. Firstly, a race over the Beacon course at Newmarket, won incidentally by a son of Gimcrack, with Sir John Moore's bay colt by Herod unplaced. A racegoer present stated, 'over a bottle of port' it is written, that this bay colt was subsequently named Highflyer. As it does not say after how many bottles of port, the evidence must be suspect! The second race in which Highflyer is alleged to have been beaten, was in a race from 'The Ditch In' won by Quicksand, 'Lord Bolingbroke's colt by Herod was unplaced'. Lord Bolingbroke owned a colt by Herod out of Marotte and it seems probable that this is the colt referred to on both occasions. The first volume of the Stud Book reads: 'Highflyer never paid forfeit and was never beaten. The author is induced to deviate thus far from his general plan, at the request of an old sportsman, from whom he learns that many bets have been made on this fact, owing to an error in the Index to the Racing Calendar of 1777, wherein Highflyer is confounded with a colt of the same age, got by Herod out of Marotte.' Well, thank heavens that horses have to be named today before they can run and that we have the Calendar and *Timeform* and *Raceform Up-to-Date et al*! Highflyer bred three Derby winners in four years: Noble, Sir Peter Teazle and Skyscraper. Rachel had another successful son in Mark Anthony, who won twenty of his twenty-eight races. He sired a Derby winner in Aimwell, the only horse to win the Derby who is not descended from the three great foundation sires – the Godolphin and Darley Arabians and the Byerley Turk. He was descended from the Alcock Arabian.

Yet another daughter of Blank bred Goldfinder, who was never beaten, and was to challenge the great Eclipse. The excitement awaiting the meeting of these two unbeaten horses for the Kings Plate in 1770 was intense, but unfortunately Goldfinder broke down at exercise shortly before the race.

The year after producing Lath, Roxana died foaling Cade, the son of the Godolphin Arabian who was to hand on the line, to be reared on cow's milk. Cade was not as good a racehorse as his full brother, Lath, but he was a very good stallion, who besides Matchem, got another branch of the line that ran for a few generations. His son Changeling got Le Sang, sire of Bourbon, winner of the St Leger, and of Duchess, winner of the Doncaster Cup; Le Sang himself was out of a mare called Duchess. Bourbon won the St Leger in 1777, the year before the classic was named after Lt General Anthony St Leger of Park Hill. Presumably the Park Hill Stakes, the equivalent of the fillies' St Leger, is named after his residence. The progeny of Le Sang ran first and second as Bourbon beat a filly Ballad Singer by Le Sang. He was ridden by a well-known Yorkshire jockey called John Cade.

Cade's famous son, Matchem, gave his name to the male line of the Godolphin Arabian just as did Eclipse to that of the Darley Arabian and Herod to that of the Byerley Turk. The name he gave to the line is often spelt Match'em but it is recorded in the General Stud Book that in 1748 the Partner Mare (Mr Crofts 1733) bred a bay colt called Matchem by Cade. Around this time they were not too particular about giving horses a name as there are ten Partner Mares in the stud book belonging to Mr Crofts and another eight belonging to other breeders! Bred way up in

Northumberland at Bywell, where Lord Allendale now lives, by William Fenwick, Matchem made a winning first appearance at York then won again in his home county. He won three times the next season and then went, unbeaten, south to Newmarket, where he beat a good horse in Trajan by Regulus, with the others distanced. In this race Trajan had shown the better speed and his defeat was put down to lack of condition, a suggestion that William Fenwick immediately countered by challenging for the Whip. The Whip, which is said to have been carried by Charles II when he rode at Newmarket, hangs over the fireplace of the coffee room in the Jockey Club rooms. Round the handle of the trophy and also in place of the keeper are hairs from the mane or tail of Eclipse. A challenge for the Whip was decided over 4¼ miles. Matchem, ridden by the Yorkshire jockey, John Singleton, started favourite but Trajan was a hard puller and went so far in front that long odds were laid on him, but Matchem got up to his opponent and went on to win easily. He won one other race before going to stud at only 5 guineas.

The first of his offspring, Caesario, proved a good one. From then on his fee went up and up to keep pace with his numerous winners year after year. He was still going strong in his old age, getting the St Leger winner, Hollandaise, when he was twenty-six and Teetotum, winner of the Oaks, when he was twenty-eight.

In 1772 his progeny won 15.5% of the stake money on offer during the season! The St Leger that Hollandaise won was the first to be run after the race had been named. She was a grey filly and was ridden by George Herring, who was later tragically killed at Hull. The Doncaster meeting should have seen a great double for Matchem as his son, Magog, also a grey, would almost certainly have won the Doncaster Cup had he not been most brutally got at by having his tongue nearly severed. The race was cancelled. Despite his injury he, like Sea Cottage who was shot in the quarters, came back to win several more races.

Pumpkin was one of the very best sons of Matchem and at Newmarket he beat Firetail and Conductor, the son of Matchem that was destined to carry on the line. Stubbs painted Pumpkin many times, being very fond of his characteristic head and face with its big blaze. Conductor was the winner of ten races. He was a chestnut and got ten foals out of a mare called Brunette, recorded as a brown filly. Five of these foals were black, among them Trumpator. A columnist who wrote under the name of 'Matchem' states that 'Matchem was a racy black horse whereas most of his well-known representatives are chestnuts.' As I have written above, Matchem is recorded in the stud book as a bay, but that is no certainty as black coat colour in the Thoroughbred is difficult to follow. Firstly, because it is sometimes mistaken for brown and vice versa and, secondly, because for some reason the colour appears to be unpopular, with the result that blacks are often registered as browns. Black is somehow associated with temperament, a belief that gentle 'Black Beauty' and those sedate plumed horses carrying people to rest have done nothing to allay (neither shies he nor is restive' as Kipling describes 'The Undertaker's Horse'). However, many of the best horses of the Godolphin line were black.

The black Trumpator stood 15.2 hh, i.e. a hand higher than his grandsire. His mating with Prunella was an alliance that had an immediate and enduring effect on the history of the Turf. Prunella, by Highflyer, is named by Dennis Craig as the greatest 'cluster' or foundation mare known to racing. Within six generations she produced among her direct descendants in the female line ten winners of the Derby, seven winners of the Oaks, three winners of the St Leger, eleven winners of the Two Thousand Guineas, and eleven winners of the One Thousand Guineas. To Trumpator she bred the wonderful mare Penelope. Not only did she win sixteen races but she proved herself a very great broodmare. She found her ideal mate in Waxy to whom she threw eleven foals and then proved her own prepotence by breeding a classic winner to Rubens.

Among the firmest believers in inbreeding to the Godolphin Arabian was the 3rd Duke of Grafton (1735–1811), for many years as enthusiastic a foxhunter as he was a racing man. While Prime Minister from 1766 to 1770 he was mercilessly pilloried by the anonymous writer of 'The Letters of Junius', who denounced him as 'profligate without gaiety'. An extraordinarily character, the Duke outraged the undemanding morals of Georgian society by flaunting his lovely mistress Nancy Parsons at the races before becoming a strict Unitarian in old age, and devoting himself to the writing of religious tracts. He mated Penelope to Waxy 'for the reason that she, being herself inbred to the Godolphin Arabian of whom there were five strains in her, would be most suitably mated if put to a horse in whom there were three strains of the Godolphin Arabian.' The Duke had a very different idea from the 'barbarians', who decried the Godolphin Arabian and described him as a Barb, as to the advisability of using horses and mares of the Godolphin line. The matings of Waxy and Penelope produced wonderful results, among them Whalebone, Web, Woful and Whisker.

Whalebone was one of the great forefathers of the Thoroughbred. He founded three great sire lines of Eclipse through his sons Camel, Defence and Sir Hercules that carry through to this day. His groom said of him, 'he was the lowest, longest and most double-jointed horse, with the best legs and the worst feet.' That well-known writer 'the Druid' agreed about his feet and says, 'Whalebone was as shabby as old Prunella herself'. He was broad and strong with a shortish neck. He stood just over 15 hh and was a mottled brown horse with an off-hind white fetlock. He won many races including the Derby of 1810. Besides the great male families he founded he bred Lapdog and Spaniel, both of whom won the Derby, and Caroline, who won the Oaks.

Web was a good broodmare and a great foundation mare. She bred Middleton, who won the Derby in 1825, and would have foaled another Derby winner in Glenartney had he not been pulled to let his stable companion, Mameluke, win. Her daughter, Filigree, was dam of Riddlesworth, winner of the Two Thousand Guineas, in 1831, and of the great mare Cobweb, who won the One Thousand Guineas and the Oaks herself in 1824 and then foaled three classic winners.

Woful was a good racehorse and sire, who won twelve races and sired fifty-eight winners before going to Germany. He got Theodore who won the St Leger in 1822. Theodore was desperately unsound and was so lame when produced for the Leger that his owner sold his book and all his chances for £200. The odds against him were fantastic: £1000 to a walking stick being laid and the official starting price was 200–1. He jumped off in front and was never headed. Woful's daughters did well winning four classics. Augusta won the Oaks in 1821, Arab the One Thousand in 1827 and Zinc both of these races in 1823.

'Whisker was as near perfection in looks as anything could be, with the exception of being a little calf-kneed', so wrote 'the Druid'. Whisker won the Derby in 1815 by a 'whisker' as he just got up in the last stride to beat General Gower's Raphael with the same owner's Busto a neck away third. Whisker was probably lucky to win the Derby, as had not Busto been sent out on a pacemaking mission, he must surely have beaten Whisker as he had done before at Newmarket. Whisker won three races the next season but was not a great racehorse and retired to stud at a modest 15 guineas which quickly rose as he made a name for himself in his new role. He founded a sire line which ran through Economy, Harkaway, and King Tom, second in the Derby and leading sire in 1870 when his son, Kingcraft, won the Derby. Harkaway is not a horse of the Godolphin line but he had more of the Arabian's blood in him than any horse standing during his generation. Two of Whisker's sons won the St Leger, The Colonel and Memnon. The Colonel also ran a dead-heat with Cadland for the Derby but lost the run-off. Whisker was a great sire of broodmares. The most famous of them was Emma, who bred two winners of the Derby in Mundig and Cotherstone and was grandam of the Triple Crown winner, West Australian, one of the greatest of the male descendants of the Godolphin.

Prunella had been a granddaughter of the Godolphin's granddaughter Rachel and when Trumpator was put to another granddaughter he got Paynator. Paynator was very similar in looks to his sire, but not so lengthy. He stood about 15.2 hh and his stock had remarkably good legs and neat muscular heads. The Paynator branch of Matchem might, but for bad luck, have carried on in tail male to this day, as it does in tail female through Bee's-Wing to several great horses, and, through her son, Newminster, in the male line of Eclipse.

Trumpator's son Paynator, who was out of a Mark Anthony mare, got a little horse standing 15 hh, Doctor Syntax. Because of his size his owner decided to have him cut as a hack for his son. It was a very hot day when the vet came so it was decided to postpone the operation. The trainer, John Lonsdale, called in and was so taken with the yearling that he persuaded his breeder to part with him. He was a horse of great character with an eye 'as full and bright as a hawk's', and a head very broad at the baseof the nose with wide flaring nostrils. His quarters fell away rather sharply from the croup and he was rather short-quartered. Mouse in colour he was remarkably short-coated, so that a brief canter would bring his veins standing out like a network. Nimrod wrote that Doctor Syntax was descended from 'our very stoutest blood'. He needed to be from 'our very stoutest blood', not only to make up for his lack of inches but because he was raced for ten years, during which time he won twenty Gold Cups. It was said of him that 'he was shod with gold cups' and an attempt was made to make this come true. He liked to make his own running and cut his opponents down. In anticipation of his eighth successive victory in the Preston Gold Cup a set of golden shoes was prepared, but he never got to wear them. Bob Johnson, his usual jockey, could not ride him. The pair had built up a legend something like Brown Jack and Steve Donoghue did in the Queen Alexandra Stakes between the two world wars. Johnson understood the old horse, who would have nothing to do with whips or spurs, and would coax him on by talking to him or in moments of extreme urgency, by hissing at him. Doctor Syntax took an instant dislike to his substitute and tried to savage him. The old horse needed to be at his best to win the Preston Gold Cup as he was opposed by two formidable rivals, both winners of the St Leger, Reveller and Jack Spigot. He was in one of his very worst moods and his new jockey could not get him to do his best and he was beaten by Reveller. Doctor Syntax finished his career by winning the Richmond Gold Cup but collapsed twenty yards past the post. He never ran again. He had been a legend in his time, always way out in front, making the running; he won twenty-four races. Despite his fame and popularity he was neglected at stud because of his small stature and uncertain temper. It was a great pity as he turned out a first-class sire and he might well have founded another line of Matchem had he gone to stud earlier.

Doctor Syntax got one in his own image, for if 'the Doctor' was the Brown Jack of his day, his daughter Bee's-Wing was the Brown

Jill of hers. She was a bay mare with black points, 'light of bone and small, but well ribbed up and had good broad hips and the sweetest of heads'. Bee's-Wing not only took after her little sire in looks but she had a deal of his temperament too, for she was a tremendous kicker in the stall, although a sweet ride. Doncaster was her favourite stamping ground. She won the Champagne Stakes, was third in the St Leger and won the Doncaster Cup in 1837, 1840, 1841 and 1842. In the year of her last victory at Doncaster her admirers wanted her to contest the Ascot Gold Cup. Her owner, William Orde, was enthusiastic about it but her jockey, Bob Johnson, was not at all keen: 'let south coom to't North if they want to be beat; not we gang to them.' Nevertheless they went and the Ascot Gold Gold joined all the other trophies. In all this wonderful mare won fifty-two races, including the Newcastle Cup in her home county six times.

Those who deplore hard racing for future broodmares might expect that the last might have been heard of Bee's-Wing when she went to stud. Apparently she was used for a hack for a bit and so was not asked to produce a foal until she was ten years old. She then bred eight foals in nine years. This wonderful mare transferred her success on the racecourse to the paddocks as her first-born, Nunnykirk, won the Two Thousand Guineas and ran second to the famous racehorse, The Flying Dutchman, in the St Leger. Nunnykirk inherited his mother's head for he is described as having 'a sweet head and a still sweeter action'. His brother, Newminster, had this good action too. Although he was not so pretty a horse as Nunnykirk, he was better ribbed up and 'he went near the ground with great leverage behind and his style of creeping along without any bustle was quite beautiful to see.' But he was such a shocking walker that there were no takers when offered for £1200. His trainer had a lot of trouble with his teeth and his feet and he had to miss the Derby and York, and even at Doncaster had not got him to his liking. Nevertheless he won the St Leger easily by three lengths. Newminster never won again but at stud, unhandicapped by his physical disabilities, he proved a great sire getting such as Hermit and Lord Clifden. Through the former was handed on the line of descent from Whalebone and through the latter was handed on a branch of Eclipse that leads to Hyperion, and it is not surprising that in those 'professional chefs-de-race' as Son-in-Law and Bayardo runs the blood of that great staying mare Bee's-Wing. In tail female are descended from Bee's-Wing numerous classic winners of this century: The Panther, Herringbone, Brown Betty, Tideway, Sunstream, Mid-Day Sun, Royal Lancer and Singapore.

The unbeaten Galopade was a son of Doctor Syntax and inherited his sire's Midas touch, for he won four Gold Cups on his only four outings. The Doctor's best son was Ralph, who inherited his sire's fine velvety skin as he seemed to have no hair except on his mane and tail. He was a cracking good two-year-old and fulfilled his promise by winning the Two Thousand Guineas in 1841. He credited Doctor Syntax with his second Ascot Gold Cup in succession when he won that race the year after Bee's-Wing's victory, but he pulled up in a desperate state of distress. Poor Ralph had been got at and he died. With him died a splendid chance of handing on another branch of the Matchem line.

The value of such horses of the calibre of Doctor Syntax and Bee's-Wing, or for that matter Brown Jack and Secretariat, cannot be assessed in the value of their winnings. Every victory they score is a moral tonic to the Turf cancelling out the bad reputation earned for it by dopers and others trying to make a quick buck.

CHAPTER 2

SORCERER

Trumpator handed on the line to Sorcerer, a black horse of size and substance standing 16.1hh, a great height for those days. He was the first foal of a mare named Young Giantess, who presumably contributed to his size. The third foal of Young Giantess was the great filly Eleanor, the first filly to complete the double in the Derby and the Oaks, then beating Trumpator's famous daughter, Penelope, at Newmarket as a four-year-old in 1802. Eleanor won twenty-nine races before retiring to stud and became an important link in the Thoroughbred chain as she bred Muley, the grandsire of Pocahontas, one of the greatest of broodmares and the only one to be included in Colonel Vuillier's dosage system. Several articles on the Matchem line state that Sorcerer was out of Giantess; this is incorrect. I have seen it stated that 'Sorcerer was inbred to Matchem to the same extent that Coronation V was to Tourbillon'. This is not so. Matchem was the paternal and maternal great grandsire of Sorcerer. The inbreeding was 3 × 3, i.e. with two free generations, not so close as the famous successful Boussac inbreeding of this century. His grandam Giantess was inbred in the same manner, 3 × 3, to the Godolphin Arabian as she was by Matchem out of a daughter of Babraham.

Sorcerer was a good racehorse and a great stallion, being the sire or grandsire of sixteen classic winners, although many of his progeny were unsound. Sorcerer got off to a quick start at stud when his daughter, Morel, won the Oaks in 1808 and Maid of the Oaks did the same the next year. According to the Duke of Grafton's trial book, Morel was used on several occasions as trial tackle for the great horse Whalebone. One trial is recorded between the filly, Whalebone and Pope. Imagine trying two Derby winners and an Oaks winner together today! It seems a pity that this race should have taken place in the privacy of the training grounds as it would have packed the stands as assuredly as a million dollar stake today. At stud Morel bred Andrew, the sire of the Derby winner Cadland.

The year that Maid of the Oaks won the race of that name, Sorcerer also got Wizard who won the Two Thousand Guineas, when it was run for the first time in 1809. After winning the Craven Stakes on his first appearance, Wizard started at odds-on for the Guineas and the Derby. In the latter race he was well clear of the field from Tattenham Corner, but Pope got up to beat him a neck. They then met in a match 'Across the Flat' at Newmarket. Christopher Wilson, the owner of Wizard had such confidence in his horse that he agreed to give Pope 3 lbs. The books did not agree with him and Pope started at 3–1 on. Wilson's view was that Pope had only just caught Wizard at Epsom and that in a match the pace was unlikely to be so good, so that his horse would beat the other for speed. He was a good judge and that was exactly what happened.

Sorcerer continued with a host of winners. 1811 was a great season for Sorcerer when he sired the winners of three classics and another son was only beaten a head in the Derby. Trophonius, who inherited his sire's black coat colour, won the Two Thousand Guineas and was made favourite for the Derby, but it was another son of Sorcerer, Magic, that featured in the finish. Two sons of Trumpator led at the distance, where Magic went clear followed by Phantom. Buckle on Phantom rode a tremendous finish and just got up in the last stride. Phantom's success was put down to jockeyship. Recompense came Sorcerer's way in the Oaks, which was won by his daughter Sorcery. At stud Sorcery dropped the Derby winner, Cadland, who was thus closely (2×3) inbred to Sorcerer, for, as written above, he was by Andrew, a son of Sorcery's first classic winner Morel.

Cadland was a most consistent horse. He won the Two Thousand Guineas and met a high-class Derby-field. The judge was unable to divide Cadland and The Colonel so the Derby was run off later in the afternoon. The Colonel had been considered a little unlucky in the race so started at a shade of odds-on. Jem Robinson made the running on Cadland and somehow induced Bill Scott to believe that Cadland was tiring. The Colonel made his effort sooner than he should have done and Cadland came again to win by a neck. Two pretty exciting finishes to a Derby in one afternoon! Racegoers certainly got their money's worth before the photo finish was invented.

The next season, that of 1829, a wonderful field turned out for the Ascot Gold Cup. It included Cadland, The Colonel, who had been bought by King George IV, Zinganee who had been amiss but had run third behind the dead-heaters in the Derby, Greenmantle, the Oaks winner, Mameluke, who had won the Derby the year before Cadland, and Bobadilla, winner of the Ascot Gold Cup the previous year. It is interesting to read a letter from Will Chifney, trainer of Zinganee, to Lord Darlington, later 1st Duke of Cleveland (1766–1842), about the prospects for the race:

'Cadland and Mameluke are good horses; the latter at times shows temper and will require the most skilful management to make him do his best amongst a field of horses, and the slightest mistake in this respect will be fateful for him. The Colonel's conformation is bad; his ribs and quarters are much too large and heavily formed and will cause him to tire; independent of this, the course is not suited to him and he will be an easy victim. Still his party are so exceedingly fond of him as to think no horse can defeat him, and they have backed him for immense sums. In the face of all this, I entertain the most contemptible opinion of him for the distance of ground. I have the best horse in England at the moment in Zinganee and, if the race is desperately run, which I hope and anticipate it will be, and my brother sends him out the last threequarters of a mile to make the pace severe, I shall be very surprised and disappointed if I do not see him win the Cup without the slightest degree of trouble, notwithstanding the powerful field of horses he has to contend against.'

Lord Darlington certainly got the information from the right source, for Zinganee duly won, from Mameluke and Cadland. The heavily backed The Colonel, of whom Chifney had a 'contemptible opinion', was unplaced. Will Chifney was a good judge of form.

To return to the year of the victory of Cadland's dam in the Oaks, Sorcerer also sired the winner of the last classic, the St Leger, in Soothsayer. He was a 'large, plain horse, deficient in quality', a chestnut, but he easily defeated a record field of twenty-four, with the Derby second, Magic, among those unplaced. At stud, Soothsayer was a successful sire; we are told that his progeny 'were for the most part big and good-looking, but rather uncertain customers'. His first classic winner was Interpreter, who won the Two Thousand Guineas in 1818. The year after Interpreter's Guineas, Soothsayers's son, Tiresias, won the Derby. Tiresias, a sound and powerful horse and a good one, led all the way and won by half a length. Even for those days there were an abnormal number of false starts, mostly inspired, and the Duke of Portland, who owned Tiresias, vowed he would never run a horse in the Derby again. He kept his word, which was not difficult as his horses were just not good enough. Tiresias was a flop at stud and it was a long time before His Grace could be persuaded that his Derby winner was not as good a stallion as he had been a racehorse.

The year after Soothsayer, Sorcerer got a black colt, Smolensko, the first horse to win the Two Thousand Guineas and the Derby. Smolensko got a good son in Jerry, a horse of remarkable size and substance and the same black colour as himself, but with a coarse head inherited through his dam. Jerry won the St Leger in 1824. In those days there seems that there was always some skullduggery afoot at the Doncaster meeting and in the St Leger in particular. We have already recorded how Magog's tongue was nearly cut off. Nimrod, in a burst of indignation, writes, 'It is the many dirty tricks, the innumerable attempts at roguery, which have lately been displayed, that have given the taint to Doncaster race-ground, which will require many years of clean fallow to get rid of.'

And so it was in Jerry's year. Jerry had won the York St Leger and arrived at Doncaster some weeks before the last of the classics. Despite the money being piled on him, Jerry's price receded in the market in such a manner that his trainer could not sleep for worrying what might be up. He started taking long walks before going to bed to try and cure his insomnia. One night, as he was walking along the Great North Road in the direction of York, he saw his jockey, Harry Edwards, in a post-chaise with a pal of the bookmaker John Gully. He had a good night's sleep and substituted Ben Smith on Jerry who sailed home by two lengths.

This story was almost repeated a hundred years later when there was a fine stink about the same race. 'Brownie' Carslake was one of the leading jockeys in the twenties and was retained by the Aga Khan. His first ride for his new patron was on Salmon Trout (by The Tetrarch) in the St Leger. 'Brownie' was reputed to be a big punter and, like all punting jockeys, was in the ribs of the bookmakers, in particular one Moe Tarsh, for a fair amount. Despite his big chance on the form book, Salmon Trout drifted and drifted in the market. Rumours were rife that his jockey had been got at. So much did they proliferate that 'Brownie' was sent for by the stewards of the Jockey Club, who told him he might be in big trouble if his mount did not run up to his form. Salmon Trout won easily. 'Brownie' admitted that he had told Moe Tarsh, a big bookmaker, that Salmon Trout would not win, but said this was because he did not believe a son of The Tetrarch could stay a mile and threequarters.

There was an amusing sequence to this a few years later. Geoffrey Gilbey, a well-known and respected racing journalist, had written some disparaging words about bookmakers, to which Moe Tarsh had taken exception. Geoffrey then invited Moe Tarsh to lunch to discuss the matter; 'The main course,' he wrote, 'will, of course, be salmon trout.' This witticism completely silenced Moe Tarsh!

Jerry's son, Jericho, got The Promised Land, a top-class racehorse who should have been a Triple Crown winner but for being messed about. He won the Two Thousand Guineas in a canter, ridden by Alfred Day. Unfortunately Alfred was already booked for the Derby, so his trainer, William Day, unable to find a suitable jockey announced that he would ride him himself. His idea was to ride The Promised Land from the front but his father and his brother John thought otherwise. William was never a good jockey and the plethora of family advice made him worse. He rode a shocking race to finish fourth in a blanket finish. The Promised Land, although only ridden by a little boy, won the Goodwood Cup easily with the Derby-second unplaced and then started at odds-on for the St Leger. Under instructions from William, Alfred Day, back in the saddle, went lengths out in front and rode the colt into the ground. Alfred returned to scale to boos and hoots. William was man enough to take the blame. Alfred, he said, had ridden to instructions and that the colt, who had easily seen out the 2½ miles at Goodwood, was short of work.

The Promised Land may be said to have been unlucky not to have been the second winner of the Triple Crown but, on the other hand, he was lucky that a colt called North Lincoln, who had beaten him as a two-year-old, and again at Newmarket the next season, had no classic engagements. Henry Custance, in his memoirs, tells how he rode against The Promised Land in the Whip, which as I wrote earlier, was run over 4¼ miles at Newmarket. There were three starters, Custance being on Special Licence, Fordham on the American horse Starke, and Sam Rogers on The Promised Land. Fordham made the running at a ridiculous pace, too fast to last over 4 miles and, when he was done with, Custance sent Special Licence, a dead stayer, to the front. Custance felt his mount change his legs and steadied him, whereupon Mat Dawson, his trainer came galloping alongside and shouted, 'Why the devil don't you go along?' This infuriated Sam Rogers on The Promised Land so he shouted at Dawson, 'What's it got to do with you? How many jockeys am I supposed to ride against?' and started a slanging match for the next furlong or so. There was a tremendous race home in which The Promised Land was beaten a short head. Both horses were so exhausted by the combination of pace and distance that they stopped dead after passing the post. Neither was any good again. At stud, The Promised Land got nothing as good as himself, but his daughter Cast Off, bred one of the greatest stayers of all time, Robert the Devil.

Robert the Devil was foaled in the same year as Bend Or. The titanic struggles between these two smashers make one of the brightest pages of turf history. Cast Off was well named for, after being barren for years, she was turned out for years before being mated to an unfashionable stallion called Bertram. The result was Robert the Devil; no oil painting, being a big, leggy, dark bay with a light neck. His rival, the Duke of Westminster's Bend Or, was a horse of exquisite quality, a burnished gold chestnut carrying what are still known as 'the Bend Or spots'.

The first meeting of these two was in the Derby. Robert the Devil was ridden by Rossiter, from whom he did not get much help, and Bend Or by a one-armed Fred Archer (one arm had an iron rod running down it and a pad on the palm, as a result of having been mauled by Mickey Idris the previous month). Robert was a long way clear into the straight as Bend Or, feeling his shins, was some way back coming down the hill to Tattenham Corner. Bend Or began making up ground right up the straight. For what happened after that we turn to those who saw the race. Edward Moorhouse (1869–1939), author of *History and Romance of the Derby* and founder of the British Bloodstock Agency, wrote:

'If Rossiter had continued to make the best of his way home, the probability is that he would have landed his mount first past the post, but at the critical moment he became bewildered and excited. Steadying his mount for a moment he looked round, and, to his amazement, found Archer almost alongside, riding his very hardest. The spectacle quite unnerved poor Rossiter. He went all to pieces. Instantly grasping the situation, Archer redoubled his efforts, and amid a scene of almost unparalleled excitement, the two horses flashed past the winning post side by side. The judge's verdict was awaited with feverish interest. Within a few moments No. 7 was displayed. Bend Or had won.'

An objection followed, oddly not for anything that occurred during the running of the race, but on the grounds that Bend Or was not by Doncaster out of Rouge Rose but was in reality a horse called Tadcaster out of Clemence. The evidence was based on a statement by a dismissed stud groom, Arnull, who might have been considered a prejudiced witness. Admittedly there were omissions regarding the markings of Bend Or but there were also other omissions in the Duke of Westminster's stud book. The facts, however, were not strong enough to warrant taking away a race, particularly a Derby, so the stewards really had no alternative but to overrule the objection. The Duke of Westminster seems to have had no doubts as, three years after the Derby, Clemence gave birth to a filly called Levity by Bend Or. It is hardly likely that the Duke should have sent Bend Or to cover his own mother.

This was the second time that the family of Grosvenor had become involved in a Bend Or controversy; the first was some six hundred years ago. Sir Robert le Grosvenor, who had served with the Black Prince in France, turned up on a battlefield bearing arms showing azure, a bend or, i.e. with a gold bar running diagonally across a blue shield. His right to bear these was challenged by Sir Richard Scrope, who claimed that he alone had the right to bear these arms. The matter was referred to a Court of Chivalry under the Constable of England, the Duke of Gloucester, who decided in Scrope's favour. However, he allowed Sir Robert le Grosvenor to wear the arms differenced with a bordure argent. This didn't satisfy Sir Richard who appealed to King Richard II, who disallowed le Grosvenor to wear a difference of the Scrope arms. Sir Robert thereupon assumed arms of azure, a garb or (a golden sheaf in non-heraldic language). The family bore these until they were entitled further, when they were granted the right to quarter them with the arms of the City of Westminster, which was a pity as the latter are 'azure, a portcullis with chains pendant or; a chief of the last thereon either side the united rose of York and Lancaster proper, a pallet of the fist charged with a cross flory between five martlets also gold,' which makes a real mess of the beautifully simple golden sheaf on a blue background.

So Robert the Devil lost the Derby by a head and failed to get it back in the steward's room, but with that he was done with losing for the season. He crossed the channel to win the Grand Prix de Paris in a canter. In pouring rain he spread-eagled the St Leger field, with Bend Or, an odds-on favourite, nearer last than first. He followed this by winning the Cesarewitch by four lengths carrying 8 stone 6 lbs, a big weight for a three-year-old, and then slammed Bend Or by ten lengths in the Champion Stakes.

Bend Or showed he was in form early the next season (that of 1881) by winning the City and Suburban at Epsom with a big weight and the rivals then met in the Epsom Gold Cup. Epsom was a track on which Bend Or had scored two big victories. George Lambton (1868–1945), fifth son of the 2nd Earl of Durham, and who between the wars trained so many classic winners for Lord Derby, tells the story of the Epsom Gold Cup somewhat dramatically in his famous book of memoirs, *Men and Horses I Have Known*:

'On the Friday of the Epsom Summer meeting 1881 Bend Or and Robert the Devil ran their great match over a mile and a half for the Epsom Gold Cup, a sight I shall never forget. When the two horses came on to the course there was a hush. Betting stopped and everybody gazed at these two champions. Robert the Devil was ridden by Tom Cannon in place of his old jockey, Rossiter. He was a great slashing bay horse slightly on the leg. In the parade he was somewhat on his toes and anxious to get on with his work, while Bend Or, a beautiful chestnut, walked sedately along with Archer on his back. The reins were loose on his neck, and when he passed the stands he actually turned his head and yawned as much as to say, "What's all this fuss about?" What a gentleman he looked. The odds were 6–4 on Robert the Devil. From the fall of the flag Cannon did all he could to cut his opponent down, but two hundred yards from home Archer brought the golden chestnut alongside and won almost easily by a neck.'

If Sir George Chetwynd (1849–1917), the owner and big gambler who was obliged to resign from the Jockey Club after his jockey Charlie Wood was warned off, is to be believed, this is rather an ingenuous view of the race for he writes:

'The chief interest on Friday was the match between Bend Or and Robert the Devil for the Epsom Gold Cup, which resulted in the victory of the Derby winner by a neck. But though I have called this "an interesting event" it scarcely was so to those behind the scenes, for Bend Or was not fit, and Robert the Devil "had a leg", the consequence was that the race was no real test of merit.'

To return to Sorcerer, another of his sons was Mulatto who sired Bloomsbury, the Derby winner of 1839. Bloomsbury was the object of contention throughout his career. There were arguments about his ownership and his breeding, there were objections and there were lawsuits. William Ridsdale, his trainer, had, the year before Bloomsbury's Derby victory, quarrelled with his patron, Lord Chesterfield, in whose name Bloomsbury was entered for the Derby. When Lord Chesterfield's horses left Ridsdale's stables, the trainer claimed Bloomsbury as his property, and up to the spring of the classic year, Lord Chesterfield was threatening to scratch the colt from all his engagements. Eventually some arrangement was made and Bloomsbury ran in the Derby.

He was something of a 'dark horse' for it was his first appearance, but he emerged from a blinding snowstorm to win at 25–1 from Deception, who two days later was to win the Oaks. Persuaded by that do-gooder, Lord George Bentinck, Fulwar Craven (he objected to being called Mister), the owner of Deception, laid an objection to Bloomsbury on the grounds that he was described as being by Mulatto, whereas in the stud book he was said to be by Tramp or Mulatto. Ridsdale satisfied the stewards that Bloomsbury was qualified to run, although the onus was really on the objector to prove that he was not. Fulwar Craven therefore applied for an injunction to prevent the stakeholders handing over the stake.

Meanwhile, Bloomsbury won the Ascot Derby and an objection followed from Lord Lichfield, owner of the second. Fulwar Craven agreed that the decision of the Jockey Club in this case should be binding also in respect of the Epsom classic. However, Lord Lichfield's witnesses were not willing to give evidence and he had to go to law to subpoena them. One cannot blame witnesses refusing to support what seems a most unsporting objection, so this objection was also overruled.

Lord George Bentinck then carried the costs of bringing an action in the courts. The case was heard at Liverpool Assizes and the jury returned a verdict in favour of the defendant, Ridsdale, a decision greeted with loud cheers. Nowadays the grounds put forward for the objection would not have been sufficient for disqualification. The rule infringed, if it was infringed (my volume IV of the General Stud Book describes Bloomsbury as by Mulatto), reads, *inter alia*, 'If the mare was covered by more than one stallion the names of all stallions must be stated.' The infringement of this rule 'may be corrected on payment of a fine of not less than 5 sovereigns, provided always that the Stewards are satisfied that there has been no fraud, and in the case of omission the horse's identity is clearly proved.'

It is odd that the breeding of Bloomsbury should be questioned for the name of his sire, Mulatto, appears in almost every pedigree today, not through the Derby winner, who went to stud in Germany, but through his daughter Martha Lynn. This great broodmare achieved particular fame as the dam of Voltigeur, who won the Derby and the St Leger in 1850 and became the sire of Vedette, the grandsire of Galopin and the great grandsire of St Simon. Voltigeur was bred in Northumberland by Robert Stephenson, who had sent Martha Lynn down to York to be covered by Voltaire. The yearling was sent to the Doncaster sales with a reserve of 350 guineas, rather a high sum for those days. According to 'the Druid', Robert Hill wanted Lord Zetland to buy him, but 'the Voltaire colts were generally heavy necked and heavy fleshed', which caused Lord Zetland to dislike him; nor did anyone else fancy him, so he was led out unsold and was subsequently bought by a farmer. Lord Zetland must have had a change of heart as he took him over. Harry Hall, who painted most of the classic winners of that period, described him as,

> 'a brown horse standing only 15 hands 3 inches in height, with a rather coarse head, small ears, muscular neck with a very good oblique shoulder, deep-girthed, high on the leg, and rather light, but with a good back and powerful quarters rather dropping towards his thin light tail.'

I have a painting by this artist, of Voltigeur, which depicts him, without any doubt, as a black. His head is held by Robert Hill and Job Marson, in the Aske spots, holds the saddle. The Epsom grandstands are in the far background. I suppose my great grandfather had it painted to celebrate his bet as recorded below.

Voltigeur ran once, winning a small race at Richmond, Yorkshire, at two years old. He was sent south to compete in the Derby followed by an entourage of North Riding farmers, who arrived in London by special train like the fans of a team in the cup final.

Voltigeur failed to impress on the downs, galloping badly 'like a lumbering coach-horse'. His supporters' spirits were further dampened when Lord Zetland, in a fury, threatened to scratch him when Weatherbys pointed out that £400 forfeits were due. This was not surprising as his breeder would not have parted with his horse, of whom he expected great things, except under the direst financial pressure. As so many of his tenants had already backed the horse and come to see him run, Lord Zetland gave way, but only after Sir William Milner (my great grandfather) had paid the forfeits due, on the Monday before the race, to protect his bet of £10,000–300. 'Volti' arrived safely at the post to win with the greatest of ease.

Voltigeur started at odds-on for the St Leger but Russborough, a 20–1 chance, forced a dead-heat and then ran him to a length in the run-off. Two days later Voltigeur came out to meet The Flying Dutchman, the winner of the Derby the previous year and a truly great horse, in the Doncaster Cup. Voltigeur had 12 lbs the best of it at weight-for-age. In addition to the weight allowance 'The Dutchman' was given a terrific gallop over the full course the day before the race for the Cup, which put him off his feed, and his jockey, Charlie Marlow, was far from sober. He jumped his horse off and rode him into the ground, Voltigeur moving up at the distance and winning by half a length. It seems that not only his jockey can be blamed for The Flying Dutchman's defeat but both his owner and trainer as well. Lord Eglington told Marlow to 'go out and make an example of him' and the horse was short of work, which was the reason for the gallop the day before.

J. B. Radcliffe wrote, 'The Dutchman's flag was hauled down for the first time and Voltigeur, amidst such a scene of excitement as an English course alone can give, was declared one of the horses of the century.' Another correspondent, however, warned in rhyme:

> Ye backers of Aske's Voltigeur, boast not too much his
>   strength!
> Though The Flying Dutchman lost the race, 'twas but
>   by half a length.
> Doubt as ye will, his heart is still as strong as Spanish steel,

And o'er Knavesmire 'gainst that verdict he will enter
an appeal.'

And so it turned out. A return match took place at the York spring
meeting, Admiral Rous handicapping The Flying Dutchman to
give Voltigeur 3½lbs more than weight-for-age. The going at York
was heavy, and heavy it can be on the Knavesmire clay. The tactics
of the Doncaster Cup were reversed and this time Flatman on the
Flying Dutchman had Voltigeur some three lengths in front as
they turned into the straight. From then on Flatman began to
overhaul the leader, and tackling him just below the distance won
by threequarters of a length. On both runs The Dutchman comes
out slightly the better horse, though nothing like so successful at
stud. The two of them did much for the Turf and 'the very
carthorses were "Dutchman" for some time after this event, while
Voltigeur became a favourite name for pointers and setters.'

Two of Sorcerer's daughters foaled classic winners, while a
third foaled a horse that ran second for the Derby, unfortunately.
I write 'unfortunately' from a personal point of view for Banshee
and her foal Osmond belonged to William Milner, father of the
Milner who punted Voltigeur. Osmond seems to have been
unlucky, as Edward Moorhouse, writing in the *Bloodstock Breeder's
Review*, records:

'There were three false starts for the Derby, in each of which
Sir William Milner's colt by Filho da Puta ran a considerable
way before he could be pulled up. What influence this had
on the actual result of the contest it is, of course, impossible
to say: but the fact remains that Osmond was placed second
to Cedric, although in the fourth and true start he did not
get well away.'

The story of the race is not given in the family history I have but
the affair is put very succinctly. It reads, 'In 1823 Sir William
Milner bought a house in Eaton Square, and there the family
went to stay to see Osmond run in the Derby the following year.
Osmond was beaten and the house was sold.'

Osmond must have been amiss for the St Leger as otherwise
he must surely have run, as the Milners were enthusiastic but

unsuccessful subscribers to this classic, having eight runners between 1815 and 1825, none of them in the first three and only one with a quotation. Apart from the lack of success attending their colours, they seem to have been equally unsuccessful punters, apart from Voltigeur. Arthur Binstead, in his book *Pitcher in Paradise*, describes how a book is made on a large ante-post betting race and draws lessons from it. 'The first thing we see is how Sir William Milner backed a dead 'un.' This was the son of the backer of Voltigeur. It was not for lack of trying or hard work that this inability to back winners has been inherited by each generation down to the present day. Sir George Chetwynd, in his *Racing Reminiscences*, describes Dudley Milner, brother of the last-named William, as

'a great student of public form, and when he first came to the races from Newmarket, where he was reading hard for an examination, he used to watch the horses through a telescope. Whenever he saw what he thought was a certainty on paper, he used to make use of the very forcible expression that "it was good enough to bet until the cows come home"; indeed I think he was the originator of the saying which is still very popular.'

The son of Sorcerer to hand on the line was Comus. Comus, the heir to Sorcerer, was a chestnut marked all over with white and black spots. He was a grand type of horse and started favourite for the Derby in 1812 in which he ran third to Octavius. He went blind from a fever, as had Sorcerer, but, in a stud career that lasted till he was rising twenty-eight, he only got one blind foal. His first season at stud was brilliant; he had sixteen colts and one filly. From this crop came the first four in the St Leger: Reveller beating Ranter, The Marshall and Masker. Four years later, the second, third and fourth were by Comus. Reveller had a fine record after his Leger success, his most famous victories being his second win in the Lancaster Gold Cup and his defeat of Doctor Syntax, when that gallant little horse tried to win the Preston Gold Cup for the eighth time in succession.

Comus got a very smart filly in Matilda. She was brilliantly ridden by Jem Robinson to win the St Leger in 1827. Going to the front she led till she was headed close home by Mameluke, belonging to the bookmaker John Gully; she came again to win by a length. In the last century the rivalry between North and South was intense and nothing was more popular than a Yorkshire victory in the St Leger. Sir Francis Doyle wrote a long poem of some a hundred and eighty lines. I quote the last four:

> 'At once from thirty thousand throats
>   Rushes the Yorkshire roar,
> And the name of the northern winner floats
>   A league from the course or more.'

The result was so popular locally that it was commemorated by 'the Matilda' clock placed over the stables at Stapleton Park near Pontefract. As a boy I well remember the clock and its silvery chimes when my grandfather's horses were trained at Stapleton.

In 1838 Comus's son, the very good-looking Grey Momus, belonging to Lord George Bentinck, won the Two Thousand Guineas, in which the whole of Newmarket thought Lord Suffield's Bamboo to be unbeatable. Bamboo was leading by several lengths at the Bushes but tired to nothing. His owner blamed the jockey, saying his horse had been ridden into the ground and challenged Lord George to a match for £1000. This was duly run, although advertised as being for £300 as Lord George Bentinck thought his father would disapprove of him betting so much. The result was the same. Grey Momus started favourite for the Derby but failed to show his form, running third to Amato. Lord George was very keen on matches and Lord Suffield was able to get his revenge when his Caravan beat Grey Momus in a match at Newmarket. Grey Momus won the Ascot Gold Cup beating Epirus and Caravan. He was a very good colt although William Day, who was riding him at Ascot, says that, with all respect to Grey Momus, the jockey on Epirus must have backed him as he shouted at him ' "Go on, go on, or we'll be beat!" and then disappeared from the front like a shooting star.'

From a daughter of Comus descend in tail female Cyllene, Prince Chevalier and many of the best horses and stallions bred by Monsieur Boussac, and in tail male the line was handed on by Humphrey Clinker. He was the biggest of the Comuses and 'as splendid a horse as ever was seen'. He made a bit of a noise and was very fast.

Humphrey Clinker got a classic winner in Rockingham who won the St Leger of 1833. His stable companion, Belshazzar, was better fancied than he was and started second favourite at 7–2 with Rockingham at 7–1. Belshazzar led all the way till close home when he gave way to the favourite, Mussulman, then Sam Darling brought Rockingham to win by a length. Rockingham also won the Doncaster Cup and the Goodwood Cup and was second in the Ascot Gold Cup. He was beaten in a race for the King's Purse that was a fiasco. Rockingham was several lengths ahead and increasing his lead and had that good horse Lucifer so well beaten that the latter's trainer shouted to his jockey to pull him up. Jem Robinson on Rockingham heard this and eased his mount. Lucifer's jockey ignored his instructions and kept at him coming at Rockingham with a rush. Jem Robinson was unable to get his horse back into his stride and was beaten a length.

In his *History of the St Leger Stakes*, J. S. Fletcher writes, 'Of Rockingham Herring painted one of his best and most characteristic studies of famous racehorses.' Rockingham must have been a very good model for when my wife and I saw one of the most lovely portraits of a Thoroughbred we have ever seen, it was of Rockingham by John Ferneley senior. With regret we left the picture in a gallery in London while we went off to Scotland, where my wife learned that she had inherited some money, enough to buy the picture. We hurried back to find it had gone, like Mahmoud and Bahram and Nasrullah and others, to America.

Rockingham, at stud, got the dam of Teddington, who won the Derby in 1851, the year of the Great Exhibition. London was crowded and, as it was wonderful day, so were Epsom Downs: the field of thirty-three was a record. Teddington, despite having sore shins a week before the race, started favourite and won in a canter. He won the Doncaster Cup the next season and the Ascot Gold Cup at five. He carried 9 stone 7 lbs when unplaced in the Cesarewitch in 1853 and the same afternoon was beaten by Kingston, both horses carrying 10 stone in the whip, yet his progeny were said to be soft; that's breeding.

The grandson of Comus to hand on the Matchem line was Humphrey Clinker's son, Melbourne . . .

CHAPTER 3

MELBOURNE
AND WEST AUSTRALIAN

Melbourne did not run as a two-year-old but raced four seasons after that winning fourteen races although he did not win a classic. He got innumerable winners, became champion sire, giving us two of the most famous horses in Turf history: the mare, Blink Bonny, and the Triple Crown winner, West Australian.

Railways played a big part in Thoroughbred breeding before the days of aeroplanes and freeways, and the advertisement of Melbourne at stud declares that Bonehill, where he stood, 'was one mile from Tamworth, where there is a railroad station'. Melbourne has been described as a horse of prodigious power. He was a rich, dark brown, his only markings being a white stripe. The Priors tell us that this last can be checked as 'his head was preserved and adorned the wall of a house in Bridlington.' He had lop ears and lacked quality and it was the sight of his knees that made a buyer turn him down when offered Melbourne along with two other Humphrey Clinker yearlings which he took. 'The Druid' tells us that 'if you go into a paddock and see a lengthy plain-headed foal with lop ears gazing at you, it may be safely set down as a Melbourne.' Despite this, Melbourne turned up to compete for the Great Yorkshire Show. It used to be the custom for stallions to appear at agricultural shows and Voltigeur stepped into the ring at Middlesbrough to win the prize for the 'Best Thoroughbred stud horse, best calculated to improve and perpetuate the breed of the sound and stout Thoroughbred horse, not only for racing, but for general purposes'.

The skeleton of Melbourne's famous daughter, Blink Bonny, is preserved in the museum at York, where it was later joined by that of Tracery. I have never learnt how Tracery got there, but it is eminently fitting that the earthly remains of a Derby and Oaks victress should be preserved in the capital city of the county of which she was the heroine. (Incidentally, I saw a skeleton of a horse in a National stud in France and, to my astonishment, it was that of Blink Bonny's full brother Blinkhoolie.)

In this century horses trained in Yorkshire have rarely been of much account and for almost any race at Newmarket and suchlike places pencillers automatically chalk up 33–1 against any horse trained north of the Trent. In my youth, the moderate performances of horses trained in Yorkshire hurt both my pocket and my patriotism but looking at what was left of Blink Bonny I could remember with pride the time when the horses trained on the Malton wolds, the Middleham moors and the Hambleton hills dominated the Turf. The winners of more than fifty classic races were trained in Yorkshire during the middle of the nineteenth century, and, in her own county, none was more esteemed than Blink Bonny. Her owner/trainer, William I'Anson the elder, had moved his string from Gullane in Scotland to the Spring Cottage Stable at Malton in about 1850.

The dam of Blink Bonny was Queen Mary, who fell in a race as a two-year-old, and was never quite the same afterwards. She was given to her trainer, William I'Anson senior, who put her to the Ascot Gold Cup winner, Lanercost, to whom she bred Haricot. Haricot was not much to look at and neither was the next foal by Mosstrooper, so I'Anson sold the mare to a farmer in Scotland. In fact, Haricot was little more than a pony and was used by the trainer as a hack. I'Anson was a heavy man and one day Haricot, carrying her welterweight, cantered clean away from a couple of racehorses, so Haricot became a racehorse herself and a good one at that. William I'Anson set off for Scotland to find Queen Mary. (Henry Custance and Edward Moorhouse, the latter probably following Custance, state that it was the discovery that Braxey, the foal by Mosstrooper, was a good one that led to the search for Queen Mary but they were mistaken). I'Anson duly returned with the mare, who was in foal to a Clydesdale, a misalliance indeed for one who was to be the ancestress of such as Hampton, Bayardo,

Lemberg, Airborne, Owen Tudor, Arctic Prince and Vieux Manoir! To think that these patricians had a relative known as Beef and Greens who was half a Clydesdale!

After Beef and Greens had been foaled, Queen Mary was sent to Melbourne and in 1854 she bred Blink Bonny. With eight victories to her credit as a two-year-old Blink Bonny was made the winter favourite for the classics the following season, but before the new year dawned there were worried heads at Malton: Blink Bonny had inherited tooth trouble from her sire. So bad was the dental fever that, at one time, her life was despaired of. 'The filly was always leaning towards the offside as if flying from some unseen fury on the near, and they only dare tie her up with a string to snap if she ran back in one of her paroxysms' (The Druid). With infinite patience the wretched filly was fed by hand and tempted with delicacies, and it was on a preparation mostly of green feed that she went to the post for the One Thousand Guineas. She looked a rake in the paddock but, in spite of this, so great was the faith in her that she started a hot-pot favourite at 5–4 on. In the race, as might have been expected, she packed up after six furlongs, beaten by lack of condition.

Blink Bonny's trouble continued unabated between the Guineas and the Derby, so that she went to the post at 20–1 at Epsom, I'Anson's hopes being pinned on her stable companion Strathnaver. It was a desperately close finish, four horses passing over the line together but wide apart so nobody knew the result until the numbers went up. Blink Bonny had won by a neck from Black Tommy, with Adamas a short head away third and Strathnaver a neck behind fourth, Arsenal fifth, Anton sixth and Wardemaske seventh, only a length and a half behind the winner. Blink Bonny, half fit, had won the Derby in record time and had, incidentally, robbed the owner of Black Tommy of a bet of £200,000–170 about his horse. Two days later Blink Bonny came out again and easily won the Oaks despite her jockey, Charlton, losing an iron. She walked over at Ascot, won the Lancashire Oaks and won again at Goodwood.

Blink Bonny picked up a lot between Goodwood and the St Leger. Her mouth was better and she started taking some crushed oats, so she was much harder in condition when she went into the paddock on the Town Moor. Despite her great improvement she was travelling badly in the market, where there was much opposition to her, chiefly from the operations of the bookmaker John Jackson and Fred Swindell, the latter laying her on behalf of the former. It also transpired that her jockey's brother-in-law would be a big loser if the filly won, not a very encouraging thought. Blink Bonny was not the only runner from Malton for trainer John Scott also saddled the One Thousand Guineas winner, Imperieuse. This filly won in a strongly run race with Blink Bonny only fourth. William I'Anson made his way to the weighing room surrounded by a hostile crowd, who were kept back by the fortuitous appearance of the prizefighters, Tom Sayers and Harry Broome.

The trainer was called before the stewards to explain Blink Bonny's disappointing run. He showed that he, himself, had had £3000 on the filly. He was unable to offer any explanation except that Charlton had not obeyed his instructions, which were to drop the filly out and come with a run at the finish. It seems unbelievable that, in spite of this, no action was taken against the jockey. Public resentment increased when Blink Bonny came out two days later to win the Park Hill Stakes in faster time than that recorded in the St Leger.

Scarth Dixon, in his book *In the North Countree*, does not attribute Blink Bonny's defeat to any malpractice but to the fast pace at which the race was run. To me, this would seem to make Charlton's disregard of his instructions to drop the filly out, which would have been the correct tactic for the filly in such a race, even more suspicious. The prolific Turf historian Fairfax-Blakeborough describes how he was shown a whip with a silver band inscribed, 'J. C. to his father W. E. after winning the Derby and the Oaks and put in mourning for the Sellinger.' The wording is, as Fairfax-Blakeborough says, cryptic. The jockey's brother-in-law was a big winner through the defeat of Blink Bonny. It is not in the nature of things to lay against one's own family's mount. This gentleman was a punter on a big scale for he took £60,000 out of the ring both times his horse, Dalby, won the Chester Cup. Finally, it was said that the bodyguard of prizefighters that materialised was laid on by John Jackson, who did not wish hi⌐ friend to come to any harm.

It is pretty certain that Charlton pulled Blink Bonny in the St Leger. Was the trainer in on the crime? It appears not, if his son can be believed. William I'Anson senior told him that, many years after the race, he had asked Fred Swindell – 'You sent me a mysterious message, Fred, the night before the St Leger, which I've never understood to this day. The message was one sentence: "Dear W., Who won't win the St Leger?" Was it a tip for me to change my jockey – or what?' Then Swindell came out with the whole story, which the old man didn't want to go into print out of respect for those who were dead and gone, and their relatives who are still alive. Briefly it was that the St Leger was arranged, at least so far as Blink Bonny's part was concerned, months before at the Ship Hotel, Brighton. This explanation may have cleared up the mystery for William I'Anson, but we are none the wiser. 'Lord Freddie', as Swindell was known, would have served racing and William I'Anson better had he told him to take a spare set of the green, straw belt colours to Doncaster for another jockey.

How great a broodmare Blink Bonny might have been had she lived longer! She only had three foals: Borealis, a filly who was third in the St Leger and is the ancestress in tail female of such as Bayardo and Lemberg, and two colts, Blair Athol and Breadalbane. Blair Athol was foaled in 1861 and had he never been born, Melbourne would still have had a grandson to win two classics in 1864, for another grandson of Melbourne, General Peel by Young Melbourne was runner-up to Blair Athol in the Derby and St Leger. It was a vintage year. General Peel won the Two Thousand Guineas for the Earl of Glasgow; he was the first decent horse that eccentric nobleman had owned and he must have had great hopes of at last winning a Derby, but there was a chestnut with a white blaze working on the wolds at Langton who was to take the place of his famous dam in the hearts of Yorkshiremen: Blair Athol, the 'best horse in the world' as Edmund Tattersall described him in an auctioneer's puff.

William I'Anson soon found he had a colt out of the ordinary and this was equally obvious to those touts who had been watching the chestnut work. Bookmaker John Jackson came forward with an offer of £7000 for him. This I'Anson refused and then Jackson suggested that Blair Athol should be scratched from the Derby so that General Peel could be backed with safety and a good price could be got about the other for the St Leger. What happened after that is not clear but when the great trainer Mat Dawson, who himself was to saddle so many more classic winners, visited Blair Athol in his box on the eve of the Derby he writes 'I thought I had never seen such a horse.' But the owner-trainer declared, almost with tears in his eyes, that he didn't know for certain whether Blair Athol would run or not. On this evidence Jackson must have had an interest in the horse or some influence over the trainer. Jackson had backed both General Peel and Blair Athol, but other bookmakers had gone for the former and laid the latter and they tried to persuade Jackson to use his influence and scratch Blair Athol. Apart from these high-level negotiations there had been other sinister machinations which might have resulted in Blair Athol not arriving at Epsom at all. The colt had been suffering from a recurrent and unexplained lameness. The reason, however, was disclosed by a conversation overheard in a barber's shop in Malton by a friend of I'Anson who was staying with him. The trainer, acting on information received, caught the boy that did him hitting the colt between his hind legs with a currycomb. Despite the belief of the bookmakers that it was a two-horse race, it was, as stated above, a vintage year. General Peel was only joint favourite with Scottish Chief, Birch Broom was a point longer, Cambuscan, unbeaten as a two-year-old, was at 6–1. The good-looking Ely, another grandson of Melbourne, and Coastal Guard were both fancied, and the two horses who had been placed in the Two Thousand Guineas behind General Peel were running again. Blair Athol, making his first appearance on a racecourse in the Derby, was at 14–1.

There was the usual trouble at the start and when they did get away Blair Athol was actually the last of the thirty runners. He was still there rounding Tattenham Corner, while General Peel, out in front, appeared to have the race in safe-keeping. Blair Athol improved all the way up the straight so that Aldcroft, on General Peel, had to get down to ride. There was no response, either General Peel was beaten or he shirked the issue, as he was to do on future occasions. Blair Athol went past him to win, going away by two lengths. On the Friday, Fille de l'Air, who had shown nothing when starting favourite for the Two Thousand Guineas, showed much better form by winning the Oaks and the French filly was the object of a hostile demonstration by the crowd. In retaliation for this, Blair Athol received a rough showing when contesting the Grand Prix de Paris the following Sunday. Blair Athol ran second. It has been said that Challoner, who rode him, would not have dared to win even if he could have done but it is more likely that Blair Athol was stale after his race at Epsom and his journey to Paris in the horse-box that had been built originally for his dam.

Blair Athol won at Ascot and Goodwood and, giving weight, finished second at York. He started favourite for the St Leger at 2–1, with General Peel at threes. As at Epsom, General Peel showed his speed and in the straight was well in front:

'But see, ere they come to the distance,
   Blair Athol comes gallantly out;
He collars the crack in a moment,
   His friends are beginning to shout!
The ghostly white face of the chestnut
   Is close to the girth of the bay;
The son of Young Melbourne is fast,
   But the son of Blink Bonny can stay.
Now, Aldcroft, lay on with your whalebone,
   And rouse up his pluck with your heel,
No – just as he did in the Derby -
   He swerves from the lash and the steel.
"The General's beat!" is the cry
   "Tis the Derby again to be seen,
Blair Athol comes home in a canter.
   Three cheers for the straw and the green!" '

So the poetically inspired correspondent of *Bell's Life* describes the finish, and, I think, very adequately. Blair Athol won by two lengths and then a tragedy occurred: as they pulled up, another horse struck into Blair Athol, deeply gashing a hind leg and injuring a tendon. The white-faced chestnut never ran again. His greatness rests, not on the number of races that he won, but the manner in which he won them and the quality of the horses that he beat. It was, as I have said, a vintage year, like that of Ormonde, Minting and The Bard and that of Mill Reef, Brigadier Gerard and My Swallow.

Many writers have stated that Blair Athol was a failure at stud. 'It was hoped that he would earn a great reputation at stud, at which, however, he proved a failure.' – Louis Henry Curzon. What does a horse have to do to be a success? He was the leading sire on four different occasions between 1872 and 1879. He got Silvio, winner of the Derby and St Leger, and the phenomenal Prince Charlie, who after winning the Two Thousand Guineas went in the wind, and confined to sprinting won ten races without defeat.

A son of Blair Athol was the unfortunate victim of a revolting and vindictive crime. The Rover by Blair Athol was an undistinguished stallion belonging to a horse and cattle dealer called David Shine. This man was bankrupt when The Rover had the misfortune, as it turned out, to be credited with being the sire of St Gatien, who dead-heated for the Derby of 1884. The value of The Rover, of course, rocketed and he became an important asset in Shine's estate. An order was issued that the horse should be delivered up and sold for the benefit of Shine's creditors. When they came to collect him the horse was found dead in his box; rather than his creditors should benefit, Shine had cut The Rover's throat. An ironical twist is that St Gatien was more likely by another horse, Rotherhill.

There was never a horse of whom so much was expected as Breadalbane, the full brother of Blair Athol. There was an air of romance about him for his incomparable mother had died giving him birth. The whole country looked forward to the classics of 1865 being won by a real champion, and so they were, but not by Breadalbane. They were won by one better even than Blair Athol, the great French horse Gladiateur, who may have been the best horse ever foaled up to that time. Among those who expected great things of Breadalbane was Henry Chaplin (1840–1923, later Viscount Chaplin), the young squire of Blankney in Lincolnshire. Then a newcomer to the Turf he was prepared to pay big sums to secure the best. Chaplin was faced with a judgment of Paris, for as well as Breadalbane, there was another son of Stockwell out of Blink Bonny's dam, Queen Mary. This colt, Broomielaw, was therefore so closely related to Breadalbane that there was nothing to choose between them on the score of breeding. Chaplin solved the problem by taking them both.

Breadalbane was a big chestnut, somewhat lacking the quality of his famous brother. According to Lady Londonderry, Chaplin's daughter, Breadalbane and Broomielaw were tried together before the Two Thousand Guineas, 'the greatest mystery hung over the trial . . . rumour had it that Broomielaw had won by three lengths. But at what weights?' Henry Custance, however, tells a different story: 'I recollect we took Lytham down to Malton to try Breadalbane for the Two Thousand Guineas. I won the trial on Lytham, a smart plater, by a length and a half, at even weights. After this we didn't think Breadalbane had much chance to win.' Despite this doubt in the minds of his connections, the exploits of Blink Bonny and Blair Athol were fresh in the minds of the public, and the racegoers gave a reception to Breadalbane similar to that which a pop-star might expect today. Such was the confidence of the public in this unknown colt that he started joint second favourite. In the race from the Dip on, it was all Gladiateur until his jockey, eased him up close home and he nearly got blown out by Archimedes. His jockey, Grimshaw, got the Frenchman going again to win by a neck. Thus Gladiateur, who suffered much at the hands of his jockey, nearly lost the Triple Crown. Breadalbane was unplaced.

Despite his defeat the support for Breadalbane continued. A poetical tipster wrote:

'The ribbon blue of '65, Squire Chaplin bears away
And Aldcroft and Breadalbane are the heroes of the day.'

His admirers in the paddock were wearing rose-coloured ties, the 'all rose' of Chaplin's colours. Both of Henry Chaplin's colts were saddled for the Derby but neither pleased the paddock critics. Broomielaw, who was a savage, resented the crowds, sweated profusely and was never in the race with a chance. Breadalbane looked dull and dry in his coat and it was said that his preparation had been hurried. He went down climbing badly and the doubts about him were justified as he was being hard driven before the top of the hill. Chaplin removed his horses from the I'Anson stable immediately. Lady Londonderry writes that while her father exonerated his jockey, who was unfairly blamed by some, 'he did not hesitate to impute blame on his trainer'. Whatever the condition of the horses neither would have ever had the remotest chance with the great Gladiateur, who won in a common canter.

Breadalbane won easily at Ascot and Goodwood but was unplaced in the St Leger, which was won by Gladiateur in the easiest possible fashion. On the Friday Gladiateur and Breadalbane met again, the Frenchman giving the son of Blink Bonny 10 lbs and toying with him. Breadalbane won two races at Newmarket and then met Gladiateur at a difference of 23 lbs in the Cambridgeshire. He was unplaced but Gladiateur, carrying 9 stone 12 lbs and giving 52 lbs to the winner should have won but for his jockey's shocking bad riding. They met again the next year in the Ascot Gold Cup. The ground was very hard and Gladiateur, who suffered from navicular disease, was more infirm than usual. Lady Londonderry describes the race,

> 'Although Grimshaw's orders were to line up with the other two, he allowed Breadalbane to pass the stand the first time round with a lead of twenty lengths, while Regalia headed Gladiateur another ten lengths. Further and further the leaders slipped away from the French horse, so much that in Swinley Bottom the gap was estimated at three hundred yards. Suddenly the amazed spectators saw that Gladiateur had been given his head and lo! the interval was gone. On he strode till he passed the post forty lengths to the good.'

Certainly Gladiateur earned the title that the French gave him of 'The Avenger of Waterloo'!

Blink Bonny was a champion and the mother of a champion, but racked always with dentition fever, pulled up in the St Leger and then suffering an early death bearing her third foal, she had more than her fair share of the bad luck that dogged all the children of Queen Mary. Balrownie, one of Queen Mary's sons, was troubled with sand-cracks and difficult to train. I'Anson tried him good enough to win the Leger but he injured a hock in the trial, he was severely kicked when running at York, and was pricked in shoeing when he met Rataplan, to whom he was third in the Manchester Tradesmen's Cup in 1854. Bloomin Heather, Blink Bonny's full sister, and founder of a great line in France that comes down to Vieux Manoir, shied at a butcher's cart on her way through London for the Oaks, slipped up on the stones and injured herself. Another son, Bonnie Scotland, nearly broke a leg as a two-year-old and could never be trained afterwards. He won the Great Prize for stallions at Cincinatti Show and was twice leading sire in America.

Melbourne's son, West Australian, founded two branches of the Matchem Line that carried on to modern times. He had a deal of the Godolphin Arabian's blood in him and was the only colt of the Matchem line to win a Derby until Captain Cuttle, Call Boy and Coronach won three in six years in the 1920s; West Australian, for good measure, won the Triple Crown. He was raced in the all-black colours of his breeder, John Bowes (1811–1885) of Streatlam Castle, Co. Durham, an industrialist of a retiring disposition who would have been Earl of Strathmore had his parents married before his birth instead of nine years after it. He was trained by John Scott, 'The Wizard of North', who saddled the winners of forty-one classics. The stable raced them big and this accentuated the lightness of West Australian's frame. He was rather long in the back and, as The Druid writes, 'he was an ordinary horse to look at when his head was out of sight'. What a beautiful head it was! And he was not an ordinary sort to go for 'he had a long stealing action that gave nothing away'.

West Australian was first tried the week after the Goodwood meeting, where Longbow had won the Stewards Cup carrying 9 stone 9 lbs. It was raining torrents in the morning, so the gallop was postponed to the afternoon when the owner and trainer had luckily had the wolds to themselves. They were the only ones to see the two-year-old trounce the winner of the Stewards Cup and Mr Bowes left Malton to catch the express at York. Before ten o'clock the next morning a commission of £1000 had gone on West Australian at 33–1 to win the Derby the following year.

'The West' was surprisingly beaten on his first appearance at

Newmarket by Speed the Plough, but three days later won by several lengths with Speed the Plough back in third place. His first run the next season was in the Two Thousand Guineas which he won easily at 6–4 on from Sittingbourne. He started at 6–4 against for the Derby but did not have things all his own way. It was a tremendous finish with Frank Butler getting the favourite home by a neck from Sittingbourne with the third only a head away.

The possibility of stopping West Australian in the St Leger exercised several minds and, in particular, that of Harry Hill, one of the less likeable bookmakers around at that time. Although the Derby winner looked a fair thing for the last of the classics, he was very easy to back, which in view of the friendship between Frank Butler and Harry Hill was not difficult to explain. As in the case of 'Brownie' Carslake and Salmon Trout seventy years later, the stewards took a hand; Lord Derby and Colonel Anson had the jockey up and warned him that he would be in serious trouble should the favourite get beaten. They then dealt with the trainer, who according to William Day, was in debt to Harry Hill. Lord Derby gave the bookmaker a cheque which severed the connection with the stable. The attempts to fix the favourite did not end there: According to a story that Frank Butler is said to have told Lord Derby about, a horse called Scythian, ridden by John Wells, was started expressly to look after West Australian. Frank Butler is said to have given a dramatic account of how he threw off the attentions of this horse and his jockey several times. Unfortunately for the truth of this tale, there was no horse running called Scythian and John Wells rode that good horse Rataplan into third place, but quite possibly another of the runners was out to spoil the chance of the favourite.

West Australian arrived at Doncaster 'looking like a bag of bones with hair as rough as a badger's'. This may well be why, as well as the rumours flying around, that he started at 6–4 against instead of on. Frank Butler was told not to win by any heads or necks and make his supporters 'shiver in their shoes; let him out at the Red House and see how far he can win.' This he did and West Australian won with the greatest of ease by three lengths. West Australian won all his races at three and continued the sequence at Ascot the next season, that of 1854, in which he won the Gold Cup in a great race by a head and a length from Kingston and Rataplan.

The stud career of West Australian has been called a failure, but had he not been a horse of such brilliance that so much was expected of him, it could have been described as highly creditable. In his first crop was an Oaks winner, Summerside, and in his next was the Two Thousand Guineas winner, The Wizard. The Wizard was out of a mare by The Cure, which might have been why his owner bought him for he belonged to Anthony Nichol, a chemist in Newcastle. He went into John Scott's stable at Malton to be trained, the same as his sire. He won his first race and then with odds of 5–1 laid on him was beaten by the appropriately named Vanquisher at York. In 1860 he started at 20–1 for the Two Thousand Guineas, which he won easily. He started at a fractionally shorter price for the Derby than Thormanby, who was out of the famous mare, Alice Hawthorn. Thormanby was sired by either Melbourne or Windhound and was owned by James Merry (1805–1877), an uncouth suspicious-minded Scot. Thormanby won ten races in fourteen outings as a two-year-old but missed the Guineas for the Derby. Henry Custance had been riding Thormanby in his work, but James Merry sent over to Russia for a jockey named Sharpe, who turned up on the course the worse for wear, having got at the sherry bottle before leaving Merry's house. Custance, at the scales, was told to put on Merry's second cap for Northern Light. Custance writes,

'When we arrived in the paddock, Mr Merry and Mathew Dawson had rather a warm argument about who were to be the respective jockeys. It ended with Sharpe and myself being told to change caps, and I donned the black one and rode Thormanby. Sharpe, on the back of Northern Light, had orders to make the running for me, but he was never in the first ten.'

The pace was very moderate until after Tattenham Corner where Nutbourne and an American horse, Umpire, went on. Nutbourne broke down badly and The Wizard went to the front to be challenged by Thormanby, who beat him on the run in.

The Wizard ran a much better race than his Derby conqueror in the St Leger, when the pace was very much faster than it had been in the Derby. The Wizard appeared to have the race in safe-keeping when he suddenly tired and was run out of it by a good stayer in St Albans, The Wizard being edged out of second place by High Treason on the post. The Wizard did very well the next year winning three Cups. He was sold for stud to Germany.

A daughter of West Australian named Lady Sefton foaled a colt, Sefton, who, in 1878, rewarded Stirling Crawfurd with a Derby, the only classic to have eluded him up till then in a long career of ownership. Edward Moorhouse tells the adventure of Lady Sefton:

'One bleak winter's evening, a young man in charge of two Thoroughbred mares ploughed his way through the snow, which covered the ground to the depth of several inches along the road leading from York to the Moorlands Stud Farm four or five miles from the city. Presently he came to a crossroad and, uncertain of the route, climbed the signpost and struck a match to read the lettering. Frightened by the flickering light of the match, the two animals started back and, gaining their liberty, dashed along the road in opposite directions. A moment later, the one answered the other's call and, joining forces, they galloped away towards York.'

The two mares were eventually recaptured and arrived safely at the stud farm to be covered.

'The following year these two mares foaled within a minute of each other. While attending to one Gilbert heard a splash in the adjoining box and went, as soon as possible, to see what was the matter. He found a newly born foal with its forelegs in a tub of water standing in the corner.'

Thus a Derby winner came into the world. In the Two Thousand Guineas, Sefton ran third to Lord Derby's famous foundation mare, Pilgrimage. In the Derby, Constable was riding a most comfortable race on Sefton a furlong out, when Goater on the French horse, Insulaire, began moving up. Fred Archer shouted a warning to Constable, 'Look out! Old Jim Goater's coming,' whereupon Constable shook Sefton up and rode him out to win by a length with Archer on Childeric third.

Another of West Australian's daughters produced Musket. Musket was late to come to hand, an unfortunate failing for a horse the property of the Earl of Glasgow, as this nobleman would gallop his yearlings and then scream 'Off with his head!' at any youngster who could not scramble over five furlongs in well under a minute. Luckily for Musket, his owner died before he could be tried. He proved a great stayer. He stood for six seasons in England without much success and he was sold to New Zealand, where he achieved fame as the sire of the great Carbine.

On the death, in 1860, of Lord Londesborough, who had bought West Australian from John Bowes, his stud was dispersed and West Australian came up for sale. The auctioneer greeted him with the cry of 'Here comes the pick of England!' as he strode into the ring with his beautiful white-blazed head held aloft. To the dismay of onlookers the highest bid came from France and 'The West' was knocked down to the bid of the Duc de Morny, a half-brother of Emperor Napoleon III. After the Duke's death, he went to the French National Stud. He sired many good winners in France including Ruy-Blas, who ran nineteen times to win fourteen races at three years old and who, at stud, got Nubienne, winner of the French Oaks and the Grand Prix de Paris in 1879.

West Australian was in France and his only classic-winning son was in Germany but it was a horse in Ireland and a foal exported to the United States that would hand on the Matchem line . . .

CHAPTER 4

ACROSS THE ATLANTIC

The Americans were quick to appreciate the value of the horses that were being bred in England from the Eastern sires and their descendants in the early days of the Thoroughbred, and took every advantage of buying stock of highest quality.

Indeed, the first Derby winner, Diomed, went there. Many successful and well-bred horses crossed the Atlantic and found that their new environment suited them, so it was only natural that with the passing of time, American-bred horses should make the opposite crossing to compete successfully on level terms. As mentioned, the American-bred Umpire was running in West Australian's Leger. The Americans' first great successes were achieved in 1881, which was known as 'the American year' through the successes of Iroquois and Foxhall.

In 1858 a suckling foal by West Australian named Millington was imported from Ireland into the States. He turned out to be a moderate racehorse, only winning a couple of races. He then had the luck to be bought, renamed Australian, and sent to stand at the famous Woodburn Stud, which sheltered the great stallion Lexington. The latter was the leading sire no less than sixteen times, so naturally Australian was set to play a second fiddle to his illustrious stable companion. Nevertheless, it is often a greater advantage for a stallion to stand as an understudy at a stud where he is ensured of well-bred mares than as lord of the harem at a little-known stud. Australian took full advantage of the chances that came his way. He got many famous sons and daughters. It was a daughter of his that gave birth to Iroquois, who, as mentioned above, was an invader of England.

Iroquois was bought by Pierre Lorillard, the tobacco millionaire son of a French emigrant, who like Sterling Clark and Paul Mellon later, raced the best of his horses in England. George Lambton writes that Pierre Lorillard 'was as great a gentleman and as good a sportsman as ever went racing'.

As a two-year-old, the dark-brown Iroquois was fairly useful, without giving any indication of being up to classic standard. The Two Thousand Guineas the following year had a most open appearance. A number of horses were well backed; not so the American colts, of whom there were three – Iroquois, his stable companion Passaic, and Mr J.R. Keene's Don Fulano. An English horse at a long price was Peregrine, although he had been backed by the stable as he had been highly tried and fancied accordingly. Peregrine was out of a mare of the Godolphin line, Adelaide by Young Melbourne. He ran up to the form he had shown in his trial and won the Two Thousand Guineas very easily from two of the American invaders, Iroquois and Don Fulano. The son of Adelaide was immediately installed as hot favourite for the Derby, but the backward condition of Iroquois had not escaped the eagle eye of Fred Archer, who had finished fifth on the second favourite Golden Plover. Archer, with Piggott-like perception, went to Jacob Pincus, the trainer of Iroquois, and asked for the mount on the colt for the Derby, to which suggestion the trainer gladly agreed.

Iroquois, as Archer had anticipated, had come on a lot by Epsom, but Peregrine maintained his position in the market and started a very short-priced favourite. The Guineas winner was a heavy-shouldered colt and not really suited by the bone-hard conditions prevailing that year. He was unable to act at all coming down the hill but, in spite of this, his jockey had him in front on the rails round Tattenham Corner. When asked for his effort in the straight, Peregrine, feeling the going, veered off the rails and Archer slipped Iroquois through on the fence to win comfortably by half a length from the favourite, with Town Moor third.

The cable which flashed across the Atlantic IROPERTOW (Iroquois – Peregrine – Town Moor) caused great excitement and enthusiasm on the other side. Business in Wall Street and the

Stock Exchange was suspended and the cheering was loud and prolonged. Fred Archer immediately became a hero in America and was offered £10,000 if he would allow himself to be exhibited over there.

Peregrine was so stumped up by the hard going that he never ran again, but Iroquois appeared at Ascot to win the Prince of Wales's Stakes and the St James's Palace Stakes. In spite of these victories he was heavily fielded against for the St Leger, chiefly because of the apparently odd training methods employed by Pincus. On the Monday before the race he put up such a rattling good gallop that his price came tumbling down and he started favourite at 2–1. He appeared at Doncaster heavily bandaged, but, in spite of the criticisms levelled at him, the American trainer had known what he was doing, for Sir George Chetwynd comments, 'considering the trouble his front legs had given his trainer, the condition of the colt reflected the highest credit on his connections.' In the race Archer tucked Iroquois in at the back of the field but moved him up to the middle by the Rifle Butts. Here they disappeared into dense fog and when they came into sight again the joint second favourite, Ishmael, was in front with Iroquois sixth, and Geologist and Lucy Glitters behind him. Entering the straight the last-named filly was raced into the lead, but, once fairly in the line for home, Archer set Iroquois alight and the race was over; the American winning cleverly by a length from Geologist with the filly third. Iroquois was beaten in the Champion stakes into third place behind the older Bend Or, but next day he won the Newmarket Derby.

Iroquois, to the regret of Sir John Astley (1828–1894), a very popular but frequently improverished member of the Jockey Club, who remarked 'he was just the type of horse I should like to breed from', returned to stud in America, where he was champion sire in 1892. He sired the two unbeaten horses, Helen Nichols and G. W. Johnson, as well as the brilliant Tammany. Iroquois was a good and game racehorse and a worthy winner of the Blue Riband in an average year, but he was extremely lucky to win in 1881 because two of the greatest horses in Turf history did not hold the classic engagements – the unbeaten Barcaldine and the other a compatriot of Iroquois – Foxhall. Barcaldine was, of course, a link in the Matchem line in England. Foxhall was not of the Matchem line in tail male but he was descended directly in tail female from Selima, the daughter of the Godolphin Arabian that had been imported into America in the reign of George II.

Foxhall in 1881 had a wonderful season, improving vastly as it went on, so that by the end he had proved himself the best three-year-old in the country, better even than his compatriot, dual classic winner as Iroquois was, and probably the best horse of any age over a middle distance; that is not to say that Foxhall did not stay, as he proved that he did when he won the Cesarewitch, but he was racing at the same time as one of the greatest stayers of the Turf, Robert the Devil. His improvement during the year was amazing. Early on he was beaten easily by Bend Or in the City and Suburban Handicap in receipt of 34 lbs (of which 20 lbs was weight-for-age), but at the end of the season he won the Cambridgeshire with Bend Or unplaced at weight-for-age. Foxhall crossed the Channel to win the Grand Prix but failed behind Robert the Devil in the Ascot Gold Cup; (Foxhall won this race the next year). He then won the Grand Duke Michael Stakes before spread-eagling the field in the Cesarewitch by twelve lengths. This victory earned him a stone penalty for the Cambridgeshire in which he carried 9 stone, a big weight for a three-year-old to carry successfully considering the quality of the field.

It is interesting to look at some of the weights (weight-for-age at that time of the year was 8 lbs) in the field of thirty-one for that Cambridgeshire of 1881 and to study the class of the runners in the big handicaps in those days, before the pattern races were staged to ease the path for class horses.

9st 8lbs BEND OR, 4 yrs – winner of the Derby
9st 0lbs FOXHALL, 3 yrs – winner of the Grand Prix de Paris
7st 9lbs TRISTAN, 3 yrs – had won Gold Vase, 2nd in Grand Prix, won both Champion S. & Hardwicke S. 3 years running
6st 13lbs WALLENSTEIN, 4 yrs – won Liverpool Cup & Manchester Cup
6st 7lbs LUCY GLITTERS, 3 yrs – 2nd Oaks, 3rd St Leger

6st 5lbs CORRIE ROY, 3 yrs – won Ebor 9–12, Manchester
Nov 9–10, Cesarewitch 8–7, Alexandra Stakes
5st 12lbs ETONA II, 3 yrs – several races, handicap with 9–4

It was a good handicap for which Bend Or started favourite, Foxhall winning by a head from Lucy Glitters, with Tristan a neck away third. The finish was fought out many times after the race; the winner being the one in which the speaker was interested. Sir George Chetwynd writes that Fordham rode a shocking race on Tristan and ought to have won. William Day, trainer of Foxhall, wrote that the best horse won and many people were fallacious in saying that Tristan was unlucky in being beat and that Foxhall was lucky to win. William I'Anson, trainer of Lucy Glitters, writes that if Martin had sat still on Lucy Glitters instead of showing her the whip, she would have won in a canter.

The most famous son of Australian and the one who handed on the line was a colt out of Aerolite, an unraced sister of the good racemare Idlewild. His owner's wife arrived back from New York with a cargo of hats and dresses and he asked her innocently if he could name a yearling after her, thus Spendthrift got his name. Spendthrift won five races as a two-year-old and Foxhall's owner, the financier James R. Keene, then bought him to go east. Keene had backed his horse, Dan Sparling, heavily to win the Withers Stakes and Spendthrift had his head pulled off to finish second half a length behind his stable companion. This aroused so much indignation with the crowd that the 'declaration to win' was later brought in. Five days later Spendthrift won the Belmont Stakes by six lengths. In his next race he put up an incredible performance. He was kicked badly and left at the post fifty yards behind the field but got up to win by a length. After winning the Jersey Derby he was then beaten twice by Falsetto, who was out of a daughter of Australian. Spendthrift was sent to England and was in the successful American team of 1881 but contracted a cold and was permanently affected in the wind.

Spendthrift was a chestnut with a diamond star and both hind pasterns white. He had a beautiful clean-cut head, deep neck, and short back, but his shoulders were a bit heavy. He had very thin-soled feet and did not like it hard. He was a great success at stud and from his first crop came Kingston, who won the almost incredible total of eighty-nine races and was only four times unplaced in a hundred and thirty-nine starts, a really good horse and twice champion sire. Another racehorse and good sire was Lamplighter. Spendthrift's name is commemorated in the famous stud. His son Hastings handed on the line.

Hastings won three of his four races at two years old and was a good and consistent racehorse, if not a great one, winning his fair share of races. He retired in 1898 to August Belmont's stud at Lexington. He was not a large horse, but with magnificently muscled quarters, rather curby hocks and a fiendish temper, which gave his handlers a big problem. He would not allow himself to be bridled and his groom, though armed with a cudgel, took chances in handling him. This was surprising, as Spendthrift had been a gentle horse. He got many precocious two-year-olds and headed the sires' list in 1902 and 1904. His best filly was Gunfire, who did not shine at two but the next season won five races, and at four was the first filly to win the Metropolitan Handicap, a record which stood for another quarter of a century. The most famous of the progeny of Hastings was Fair Play.

Fair Play won three of his first four starts but then lost six in a row. Colin was much his superior. At three, Colin broke down and so did Celt leaving Fair Play as the best of his age. The importation of Rock Sand by August Belmont helped pave the way for the most outstanding stud successes of Fair Play, who nicked well with the daughters of the English Triple Crown winner. Rock Sand himself also suited Fair Play's distaff blood, for when he was mated to Fair Play's dam the result was Friar Rock, the best three-year-old of his year. Fair Play had a wonderful record at stud, heading the sires' list in 1920, 1924 and 1927, in which last year he would have broken the record for winning stakes if his own son had not set up a new record the previous year. Three of his sons, Chatterton, Chance Play and Man o'War, themselves headed the sires' list.

Apart from the peerless Man o'War, the best son of Fair Play was probably Mad Hatter, who like Man o'War, was out of a Rock Sand mare. Mad Hatter, unlike Man o'War, was a bay. He had a long and strenuous racing career extending over six years during which he won thirty-two races and was second twenty-two times. He was born the year before Man o'War and was a contemporary of Friar Rock. He was a most versatile performer, winning at all distances from six furlongs to two miles. He was sold as a stallion to Harry Payne Whitney, his best son being The Nut.

Display heads the list of Fair Play's stake winners and was described as 'the iron horse'. He contested many races although he was a very difficult horse to handle, with a very bad disposition, and was quite mad at the barrier. He won the Preakness in 1926 and twenty-two other races and was placed fifty-two times. Display got a typical scion of his line in Discovery, a golden chestnut standing 16.1 hh. Discovery was one of the great weight-carrying handicappers of the American Turf. He was slow to mature and only won two races in fourteen outings as a two-year-old. This seems a lot of appearances for a backward juvenile but evidently the Americans, like Yorkshiremen, must have believed that 'if they've got to gallop let 'em gallop for brass'. He must have been a promising sort for Alfred G. Vanderbbilt bought him at the end of the season. Next year, Discovery won the Brooklyn Handicap by six lengths, followed by five other races. Cavalcade appeared to be the best of the three-year-olds that season, but, when he broke down, the way was cleared for Discovery to take the crown over in the same manner as Fair Play had done after Colin's breakdown. The next year, Discovery broke the American record for nine furlongs when he won the Brooklyn Handicap for the second time, and seven wins off the reel followed that season, including the Citizens' Handicap. In this race Discovery carried 9 stone 13 lbs, the highest weight to be carried successfully in a top class American handicap since Whisk Broom had done the same in the Citizens' Handicap some years before. He scored a hat-trick in the Brooklyn Handicap and then five other races to retire with a total of twenty-six wins.

Discovery retired to stud for his name to appear in the pedigrees of nearly all the best horses racing today as he became the maternal grandsire of Native Dancer and Bold Ruler. Geisha was not a good racemare, being placed and winning a maiden, but she supplied Native Dancer's grey coat and from her he also inherited the strength and size of Discovery. The well-named Native

Dancer, by Polynesian, won twenty-one of twenty-two races and was second in the other. He won all nine of his races at two years old, including the Futurity in which he was shut in but forced his way between two beaten horses to equal the world's record for a straight six and a half furlongs. He started off his classic year by two wins, both as usual at odds on, then came the Kentucky Derby, his only defeat. Coming round the last turn he was on the rails behind a wall of horses. In the straight he burst through but failed by a head to catch Dark Star, who had led from the start. Only one opponent appeared to take him on in the Withers, which Native Dancer won at 20–1 on and went on to win the Preakness and the Belmont, the last two classics of 1953. Native Dancer was a truly great racehorse and as a stallion his sons and his grandsons are among the pillars of the stud book, while his daughter bred the all-conquering stallion, Northern Dancer. Mr Prospector, his grandson by Raise a Native, has been tipped by Bill Oppenheim in *Racing Up-Date* to inherit the crown from Northern Dancer.

Miss Disco inherited the toughness of her sire, Discovery, winning ten races in fifty-four starts. Her son, Bold Ruler, was in the wars as a two-year-old. In his first race, he swerved at the start and strained his back muscles. Nevertheless he won by a good margin, only a fifth of a second outside the track record. Then, next time out, he struck his head against the gate and finished second, bleeding at the mouth. He went on to win the Futurity and finished the season with seven wins to his credit. At three, he ran against General Duke four times. In the third meeting he beat General Duke by a neck in a track record for the Flamingo Stakes, the tables being reversed by a length and a half in the Florida Derby in what was a world-record time for nine furlongs. General Duke then met with an accident so the way should have been cleared for Bold Ruler, but another rival appeared in Gallant Man, whom he beat by a whisker in the Wood Memorial in a track-record time. He was carried out at the first turn in his next race and would not come from behind, but, allowed to stride along in front in the 1957 Preakness, he won. This made him favourite for the Belmont, although doubts were expressed as to his ability to see out a mile and a half. Knowing that Bold Ruler would do his best only if allowed to go up in front, the trainer of Gallant Man started two pacemakers. First one and then the other ran Bold Ruler off his feet (they ran ten furlongs in Whirlaway's record time for the Kentucky Derby) and Gallant Man beat him by twelve lengths in a new record time for the last of the classics. Altogether Bold Ruler won twenty-three races and retired to become a really great sire, imparting speed into the Thoroughbred and a bit of his sire Nasrullah's temperament as well. The success of his two-year-olds have led to the idea being current that Bold Ruler was purely a sire of sprinters, but Raymond G. Wilson, in his book *Secretariat*, points out that a considerable number of his sons and daughters won at a mile and a quarter, which is the distance of the Kentucky Derby, or more. He headed the sires' list again and again, while the deeds of his son, the Triple Crown winner of 1973, Secretariat, made his name known worldwide. Secretariat was bred to the purple: he had a great sire and dam, he had two great stallions and a great broodmare as grandparents, but I can't help but believe that his big frame, his chestnut colour with markings, his stockings and his stripe, like those of Hurry On and Man o'War, must be attributed to the Matchem line. These three, if not *the* three best, must be three of the best four horses to race in this century, if not ever. A decade or so ago the sons of Bold Ruler were sought after in the same manner as those of Northern Dancer today.

Among Discovery's daughters were Good Thing, dam of the smashing filly Bed o'Roses, and Traffic Court, dam of the classic Hasty Road, winner of the Preakness in 1954.

Chance Shot and Chance Play were other high stakes sons of Fair Play. The former was away to a good start and, although he only had thirty mares in his first two seasons, he had two good colts in each of those crops: Peace Chance, winner of the Belmont Stakes in 1934 and Chance Son, who won the Futurity. He was also sire of Armful, dam of the good gelding Armed. Armed did not find winning form until he was four years old but he then became one of the great weight-carrying handicappers, winning forty-one races. Chance Play's son, Some Chance, was a successful sire; among his sons was Quiet Step, who beat Tom Fool in the Roamer Handicap.

Fair Play had numerous daughters who turned out to be good

matrons, such as Beautiful Lady, dam of Sun Beau, holder in his time of the record stakes earnings, and Mlle Dazie, who bred Jamestown. Sun Beau was a huge horse standing only a fraction under 17 hh. Naturally he was slow to mature and did not get into this stride until his late three-year-old days, after which he won sixteen top-class handicaps including the Hawthorne Cup three times in succession. He held the record as the highest stake earner up to his time, and was handled by ten different trainers during his career! Jamestown was the best two-year-old of his year, and what a year it was as it included two smashers in Equipoise (great grandfather of Damon Runyon's 'horse right here!') and Twenty Grand. Next season he won the Withers but then lost his form.

When Fair Play got Man o'War out of Mahubah by Rock Sand, he got one of the few with claims to be the best racehorse ever foaled. Man o'War was born shortly before the United States entered the First World War and by the time he was a yearling his breeder, August Belmont, had become Major Belmont, so his yearlings were put up for sale at Saratoga, where Man o'War became the property of Samuel D. Riddle. He was a big-framed, upstanding, bright chestnut with a white star. Typical of his line in looks, he also had the uncertain temperament of his English cousin, Hurry On, which was to result in him forfeiting an unbeaten record. He ran ten times as a two-year-old in 1918, winning nine races. It was in the Sanford Memorial Stakes at Saratoga that he suffered his defeat, in much the same way that nearly proved the undoing of The Tetrarch, as he was left at the post. Carrying 9 stone 4 lbs and a hot favourite at odds on, he whipped round at the start, and from then on was in trouble all the way. He had a very rough passage and was finally 'blocked in the stretch'; even so, when switched to the outside he only just failed to catch the winner, appropriately named Upset, to whom he was conceding a stone. At three, he became a legend, not only in the States, where he was affectionately known as 'Big Red', but all over the world. He won the Preakness, the Withers, the Belmont, the Stuyvesant Handicap, the Dwyer, the Miller, the Travers, the Realization, the Jockey Club Cup, the Potomac Handicap and the Kenilworth Handicap. Only once in all these races was he extended, that was in the Dwyer when a very fast colt, John P. Grier, in receipt of 18 lbs showed in front a furlong out, but Man o'War came away to break the American record for nine furlongs. As the season went on older horses would race against him, so he met Sir Barton, the best of the four-year-olds, at weight-for-age for the Kenilworth Gold Cup; he won in a canter by twenty lengths. The great horse then retired with a record of twenty wins in twenty-one outings, with earnings of $249,465.

Racing men may discuss at length which is the best horse they have ever seen, not many can have seen Man o'War, Hurry On, Ribot and Secretariat. Of these, taking a racing career together with a stud career, Man o'War's only rival could only have been Hurry On. It may well be argued that Man o'War did not race beyond three years old and that when he so easily beat the older horse, Sir Barton, the latter was not completely sound, but his claim as champion of champions rests on the manner in which he beat his opponents and the times he recorded in so doing. However one may deprecate the time test as a method of assessing the merit of racehorses, a horse that could consistently treat the clock with the contempt that Man o'War did must be something of a phenomenon. At a mile he won the Withers, comfortably beating the American record; at nine furlongs he won the Dwyer, carrying 9 stone he beat the American record; at a mile and a quarter he won the Travers, carrying 9 stone and breaking the world record; at eleven furlongs he won the Belmont by twenty lengths, carrying 9 stone and breaking the world record; at a mile and a half he lost his only opponent in the Jockey Club Cup to break the American record; at a mile and five furlongs he won the Realization carrying 9 stone, by a hundred lengths, breaking the world record in 2 minutes 40 $\frac{2}{5}$ seconds. Apart from the times Man o'War recorded, his form performances were outstanding. When he won the Potomac Handicap with 9 stone 12 lbs he beat a good horse in Wildair, to whom he was conceding 30 lbs and the winner of that year's Kentucky Derby, Paul Jones, to whom he was giving 26 lbs.

When he retired to stud Man o'War was as quick off the mark as Hurry On, the champion of the Matchem line in England, and, like him, got a champion from his very first mare, for from Lady Confey, he got American Flag to win, among other races, the Belmont in 1925, the Dwyer and the Withers. In his second crop he got Crusader, a beautiful-looking colt, a little lacking rein. He won eighteen races, including the Belmont, and the Coney Island Derby beating Fair Play's son, Display. Crusader was a failure at stud.

CHAPTER 5

SOLON

Solon, the son of West Australian that handed on the Matchem line in Europe, has been treated contemptuously by many Turf historians. He has been written off as a roarer and an indifferent performer. In actual fact, he won more races than he lost and John Osborne describes him, not as an indifferent but as an 'excellent performer'. Bred in Ireland, he was big and slow to come to hand but at three years old won seven of his twelve races on both sides of the Irish Sea. The next season he won two of his three races, and in the Cesarewitch, the one in which he was beaten, he showed up for a long way. At stud he founded two branches of the Matchem line that stretch down well into this century for, as well as being the sire of the unbeaten Barcaldine, ancestor of three Derby winners, he sired Arbitrator, grandsire of the St Leger winner Kilwarlin and tail male ancestor of Zev, victor of the famous match with Papyrus. Arbitrator also got St Kevin and Theodolite, both of whom won the Irish Derby.

Kilwarlin had won no race of any account until the St Leger for which he had been highly tried and backed to favouritism in 1887. He played up on the parade and had to be led to the start, where a stable lad with a stock whip stood behind to ensure that he jumped off. This he did, but it was a false start and the next time he stuck his toes in and was still there when the rest of the field had gone half a furlong. Luckily they dawdled along which enabled Jack Robinson, who rode with admirable judgment, to get Kilwarlin up to the field without bustling him, the whole incident being repeated in the St Leger of 1972 with Lester Piggott on

Boucher. Sir George Chetwynd writes 'I could hardly believe my eyes when I saw Kilwarlin with the leading group at the bend.' It was a muddling finish. Timothy veered over to the outside, closing the gap through which Watts on the Derby winner, Merry Hampton, was coming. Watts continued his course knocking Eirispord out of the race. Kilwarlin won by half a length from Merry Hampton, with Timothy a head away third with Phil, galloping faster than anything, a neck behind him. Kilwarlin died three years later but not before he added a link that was to lead to one of the greatest stories of Turf history.

His son, Kroonstad, was a staying handicapper who once changed hands after winning a seller. At stud he bred a mare who, mated to Jackdaw, threw a brown foal destined to be known far beyond the boundaries of the racecourse as Brown Jack.

No horse of the present century, not even Brigadier Gerard, has aroused the public's adoration as did Brown Jack. For seven years the partnership of Steve Donoghue and Brown Jack were there or thereabouts in the major staying handicaps and the small punters were on him to a man, knowing full well that they would get a great run for their money. In all Brown Jack won twenty-five races and was second nine times. Of these victories, seven were over hurdles. Brown Jack was only unplaced once in ten outings under National Hunt rules. He is best remembered for his feats at Ascot, where, after winning the Ascot Stakes as a four-year-old, he won the Queen Alexandra Stakes six years off the reel. By the time of his final victory, the combination of horse and rider, both of an age past usual retirement, had become a legend of invincibility. Once it was seen that Steve had got the measure of Gordon Richards on Loosestrife in 1934, the cheering on the stands knew no bounds, continuing as he stood in the winner's enclosure that he knew so well. A whole book has been devoted to him, suffice to say here that he earned his place with the immortals and I end by quoting John Hislop's obituary in *The Observer:*

'And so, Brown Jack is no more. That brave old heart has ceased to beat, that noble head is laid to rest, for all we know, to join his old partner, Steve Donoghue, who slipped out of this life a few years back with the same quiet unobtrusiveness that marked his character when he was alive. Thus ends a chapter of Turf history, since Donoghue was the best jockey of his generation and Brown Jack the most popular horse of his time.

'To posterity it may seem strange that Brown Jack was held in such esteem by the racing public, for, though he was a good racehorse, he was no St Simon, and while his conformation was good from a practical point of view, he boasted neither the quality and symmetry of a Hyperion, nor the strength or magnificence of a Gold Bridge, nor were his victories won with the meteoric brilliance of a Tetrarch.' [Nor, if I might add to Hislop's words, the perfection of a Brigadier Gerard.]

'He earned his place in the hearts of the racing world through his individuality, his character, and the qualities of courage, honesty, intelligence, and kindness, which he steadfastly maintained throughout his long career; he could always be relied upon to do his best, to battle to the end, and to endure the attentions of his admirers with gentle good-humoured tolerance.

'Year after year he upheld the prestige of England against younger French invaders in the Queen Alexandra Stakes at Ascot, and while the whole assembly cheered him as a conqueror over France, to many a punter it meant the difference between remaining on the turf and a single ticket to foreign lands. It is to the credit of all planning his racing career that he was retired from racing before his powers waned. Although he became more bent at the knee each year, and the silent foot of age crept gradually but perceptibly nearer, he kept his form to the end, and when he was led in after his last race, his sixth successive Queen Alexandra Stakes, the applause that greeted him and his rider was mingled with joy at the knowledge that he was going to pass into honourable retirement.

'From his retirement he has gone to a deeper rest, remembered by the racing world as a good stayer, a game horse, and above all a trusted friend.'

I am thankful that I was there on that last day at Ascot, and of the many hundreds of racing days that I have seen, it is one that I have always remembered.

Another son of Kilwarlin travelled to America inside his mother. The foal, Ogden, was a good racehorse winning fifteen races, including the Futurity among other valuable races. At four, Ogden went to stud and after two years in that capacity was put back into training; at seven years old he won six races off the reel. At stud, he got several good racehorses including The Finn, Captain Alcock and Sir Martin.

Sir Martin was the best two-year-old of his year in the United States and was bought by Louis Winans with the express purpose of winning the Blue Riband. The Derby that year, 1909, was a memorable race, both for the incidents in running, the finish and a Royal victory. Sir Martin crossed the Atlantic and was made favourite at a fractionally shorter price than King Edward VII's Minoru, who had won the Two Thousand Guineas in which the great Bayardo, third favourite for the Derby had been beaten for the first time in his career. Bayardo had been far from his best and had only been run in the Guineas at the insistence of his owner, his shelly feet having given his trainer much trouble. For the Derby, however, despite a hurried preparation he stripped in magnificent condition and Richard Marsh, the trainer of Minoru, writes 'I had not seen Bayardo between the day of the Two Thousand Guineas and his appearance at Epsom, and I must say I was impressed with the marked improvement in him. He looked a different horse and the sight of him set my anxieties alight again.' Sir Martin also gained the admiration of the critics and, on looks, he did not disgrace his position as favourite. As things turned out, he was not able to show whether his merit lived up to his looks, as coming down the hill to Tattenham Corner Sir Martin came down. Bayardo, racing behind him had to be snatched up. Louviers led them into the straight on the rails but moved slightly off the fence, which allowed Herbert Jones to push Minoru through the gap. A desperate race ensued. Minoru led for a few strides . . . a furlong out Louviers got his head in front . . . then a hundred yards from home Minoru once more got his nose in front . . . but Louviers rallied and came again. Two strides past the post he had headed Minoru again, but to tell which had passed the post first would really have needed a photo-finish camera and the closest scrutiny of a film. However, in those days it was left to the judge's eye to decide. Number One went into the frame. The King had won the Derby! The Monarchy and the Derby are so uniquely British that a royal victory rivals a Waterloo or a Trafalgar. Pandemonium broke out; the crowd surged on to the course. A music-hall singer started up the national anthem, which was taken up first on the stands and then by the crowds on the Downs.

Would Sir Martin or Bayardo have won but for the accident? Sidney Galtrey, who wrote as Hotspur for the *Daily Telegraph*, writes, 'That year there was a favourite in the American horse, Sir Martin . . . Would he have justified his favouritism? Personally, I doubt it.' George Lambton writes, 'I shall always think that if Sir Martin had not fallen in Minoru's Derby, he would have won for Mr Winans and Cannon. I am sure he was a really good horse, and never completely recovered from effects of the fall although he won good races afterwards.' So you can take your own choice.

On subsequent form it seems that the King, Minoru and the crowd were lucky as Bayardo went on to win the St Leger, with Minoru fourth. Bayardo won twenty-two of his twenty-five races. Sir Martin won twice at Newmarket and crossed to France to win the Grand Prix de Trouville-Deauville and, next season won the Coronation Cup by one and a half lengths and four lengths from Bachelor's Double and the Derby second, Louviers, but finished behind Bayardo in the Ascot Gold Cup on his only other outing. At stud, Sir Martin got some useful winners but nothing anything like as good as himself.

Ogden's best son at stud was a black horse called The Finn. He broke the track record at Aqueduct in the first race he won, then, after winning another race and running a couple of seconds, he was sold to Louis Winans, the same man who had bought Sir Martin to win the Derby. He had no more luck with The Finn as, running in the Futurity, he swerved into the rails and unseated his jockey. That was the only race The Finn ran in Winans's colours as he got rid of him, so he must have felt pretty sick when, the next season (1915), The Finn won both the Withers and the Belmont. At four he broke the track record at Saratoga and won the Metropolitan. The Finn was leading sire in 1923 due to the then record earnings of his son Zev.

Zev was a useful two-year-old but it was in the following year, 1923, that he really came into his own, winning twelve times in fourteen starts, including the Kentucky Derby. In all he won twenty-three races making him the record stakes winner in the world up to that date. Zev's international fame came, not from the money he won, but from his match with the Derby winner, Papyrus. Papyrus was also an offspring of the Matchem line as his dam was by Marcovil. Papyrus was a dark brown colt, a well-muscled close-coupled horse, with a star on his handsome head. He was a really beautiful horse, as might be expected from a son of Tracery. He had a delightful temperament and was a gentleman in every way. When I was a schoolboy I saw him crossing the Knavesmire from the stables in Dringhouses with his elegant head held high, to run in the Duke of York Stakes. Just as I have never forgotten seeing the beautiful Friar Marcus out at walk, I have never forgotten the sight of Papyrus fifty-five years ago, although I have forgotten the race, which is surprising as it was a most sensational one. Papyrus got the race, though finishing a short head behind Craig Eleyr and a head in front of the odds on favourite, the lovely filly Concertina. Craig Eleyr was disqualified for boring and not keeping a straight course.

Papyrus was bought at the Doncaster sales by Ben Irish, a Northamptonshire vegetable farmer, whose racing career was a fascinating example of the great game. His first racehorse, Periosteum, he bought was a yearling for 260 guineas: it won the Ascot Gold Cup. He paid ten times as much for Papyrus but he won the Derby. It is as easy as that if the luck runs right!

Papyrus ran fourth in the Two Thousand Guineas in 1923 and then won the Chester Vase, showing that he could stay a mile and a half and that he would be capable of negotiating the Epsom turns. The favourite for the Derby was Town Guard, whom Papyrus had beaten as a two-year-old, while second favourite was a horse destined to achieve world fame at stud, Pharos. Papyrus was third favourite but, with the public, 'Papeeris', as they called him, was most in favour for he was ridden by the popular Steve Donoghue, who was attempting the hitherto unaccomplished feat of riding three Derby winners in succession. As they went through the crowd to the start, they gave Steve the reception to which his Derby victories entitled him, but Papyrus, looking in splendid condition, never turned a hair at the cheers of the crowd. Steve, confident in his mount's stamina, sent him into the lead from Tattenham Corner and from then on it was a match with Pharos, who got his head in front two furlongs out. Papyrus, responding gallantly to Steve's urgings, pulled away to win by a length from Pharos, who ran a great race at a distance beyond his best. The winner and his jockey received a tumultuous welcome from the delighted crowd.

Then came the challenge from America for him to race there against their best three-year-old, over a mile and a half at Belmont Park, for a prize of £20,000 (plus a gold cup presented by the American Jockey Club) to the winner and £3,000 to the loser. The challenge was accepted. Before leaving for America, Papyrus was beaten in the St Leger by the filly Tranquil, the One Thousand Guineas winner. The Derby winner suffered a rough passage in the race and was cut into. This defeat of Papyrus rather disappointed the promoters of the international match, but it was still with the reputation of being the best three-year-old colt in England that Papyrus sailed on the *Olympic* for New York.

From the remarks of the critics of this match, and there were many, it might have been thought that the crossing of the Atlantic was as hazardous as it had been in the days of Christopher Colombus. The conservatives considered it ridiculous that Papyrus should be thought to have any chance at all on the dead flat dirt track that he would encounter in the States. This view came, oddly enough, from those who were foremost in maintaining that the supremacy of the British Thoroughbred was chiefly due to its ability to adapt itself to any conditions or any type of course (except, apparently, a perfectly fair flat one!). Papyrus soon showed that these doubts were rubbish by doing a gallop over the full distance in a time which, to the amazement of the clockers, equalled the great Man o'War's record. The American experts frankly admitted that Zev could not have clocked a similar time but against that there was the chance that Papyrus could suddenly go flat, affected by the change of climate.

Twenty-four hours before the match it looked wide open, with Papyrus at slight odds-on. Then it started to rain. The track became a quagmire; we are told it looked like French mustard. Basil Jarvis, the trainer of Papyrus, was now in a terrible dilemma. Sidney Galtrey relates how Andrew Joyner, who had backed Papyrus on the strength of his gallop, came to him in a great state of agitation. Basil Jarvis had declined to take the advice of the Americans to have his horse specially plated so that he could get a grip in the soft going.

'Without grippers no horse could possibly extend himself. It would be unfair to expect him to do so. "Basil," he said, "won't do as I have told him. If this horse goes out in English shoes he hasn't a million to one chance; he might as well have stayed at home. He won't see the way Zev goes . . ."

Jarvis said, "They might be right, but I can't take the risk. Papyrus has never worn such plates before. He might cut a tendon then I should be blamed. I've got to think of Mr Irish and his horse."

Joyner was right to the letter. I could see the moment Papyrus got on to the track and first trotted and then cantered to the post, that he was all at sea. He would sprawl and get unbalanced the moment any pressure was applied.'

Zev now went to odds-on.

Steve Donoghue and Earle Sande on Zev, agreed with the starter that neither should attempt to gain any advantage at the start. Papyrus jumped first and Steve immediately reined back to Zev, who then went on. Steve writes,

'I was wrong. I should have stayed in front and, as soon as Zev passed me, I saw how wrong I was. Immediately he was in front he gave me everything that four flying hooves galloping through mud can give and I was riding into a hail of mud . . . I knew I had not got a chance in a million because every time the horse put out a foot it came back to within a few inches of where he had lifted it. He was just scrambling and slipping hopelessly in the mud.'

He asked Papyrus to close the gap, which slowly he did, but when

Earle Sande shook Zev up he went away to win by six lengths. As Donoghue writes,

> 'It was absurd from the start . . . if the going had been hard and the weather dry, I believe, and so does every expert here, that Papyrus would have won easily. The time he put up in the practice gallop proves that. Zev had never done that sort of time, and when Papyrus made it he was merely having an exercise gallop. Zev's own trainer agreed with me.'

And so defeated by the weather, Papyrus returned across the Atlantic to the chorus of the carping critics, 'We told you so'. But it was a fine sporting effort and I am thankful that I was racing while it was at its top, when it was still a sport, and not a business, for most of those who owned racehorses, and it was still run for the enjoyment and entertainment of racegoers.

Barcaldine, the son of Solon out of Ballyroe, who is the next link in the British branch of the Matchem line, was a truly great Thoroughbred, both on looks and performance. He was bred in Ireland by a Scotsman, George Low. The dam of Solon, Darling's Dam, was also the grandam of Ballyroe, so Barcaldine was closely inbred to Darling's Dam 2 x 3, that is with only one free generation. The Scotsman neglected to subscribe to any of the classics with Barcaldine, otherwise the 'American Year' might never have been and Iroquois would have had to sacrifice his classic victories to Barcaldine.

Barcaldine was a horse of great size and substance, a magnificent specimen of his race, but he had a mental kink and was a very bad-tempered horse. He was highly tried as a two-year-old and easily won his four races. The next year, giving lumps of weight away all round, he won the Baldoyle Derby and became favourite for the Northumberland Plate, his first engagement in England. The enterprising Mr Low then decided that there were other ways of making money out of owning a good horse besides winning races, so he sent a telegram to Sir John Astley, the owner of a fancied candidate for 'The Pitmen's Derby', asking him for £1000 in return for which he would scratch his own horse. As an alternative he suggested that if 'The Mate', as Sir John was known, could not find the necessary money, for 'The Mate' was often short of the ready, he should get 12–1 to £100 for Low about the Irish horse's chances of winning. Not surprisingly, Sir John put the telegram in front of the stewards of the Jockey Club, who refused to allow Barcaldine to run in England in George Low's colours. Low consequently put his horse up to auction, but rumours were around that he had inherited a wind infirmity from his maternal grandsire, Belladrum. One who believed this was the man described by trainer John Porter, who had sent him to look at the horse for the Duke of Portland, as 'the damn fool who didn't buy Barcaldine'. Barcaldine failed to reach the reserve placed on him and went on to win three more races in Ireland before the trainer, Robert Peck, bought him privately. Born at Malton, Yorkshire, Robert Peck (1845–1899) had trained the Derby winners Doncaster and Bend Or in the Russley Park Stable near Lambourn. He subsequently had Barcaldine and his other horses trained by James Hopper at Beverley House, Newcastle.

Barcaldine's first appearance in England was to have been in the Cambridgeshire but he was scratched by mistake and so he did not run till he was five. Robert Peck, his usually very astute owner, then made a bad error of judgment. Barcaldine was unfit and very much on the big size when he contested the Westminster Cup at Kempton Park, and furthermore he was opposing that good horse Tristan, who had won both the Champion Stakes and the Hardwicke Stakes three years in succession as well as the Ascot Gold Cup and who, it will be remembered, had been involved in that desperate close finish for the Cambridgeshire with the American horse, Foxhall. Thus Peck did not think much of the chances of his horse who started at 10–1 in a field of four. Unfit, unbacked and unfancied, Barcaldine won the Westminster Cup in a canter. As far as the handicapper was concerned 'the fat was in the fire', as George Lambton puts it, and it was with a very big weight that he won a free handicap at Epsom later in May. He followed this up by winning at Ascot.

He had been backed to win a fortune in the Northumberland Plate but he arrived back so sore from Ascot that it was only possible to give him walking exercise and just one gallop on the eve of the race. Baron de Gelsey, in an article on 'Unbeaten

Horses' in the *British Racehorse*, writes that the horse broke down as the result of his trial gallop for the Northumberland Plate.

> 'Peck, who stood to win a fortune in the Northumberland Plate in which Barcaldine had, of course, to carry top-weight, tried the horse with Harkness, who had won the Cambridgeshire the previous year by three lengths. It is said that in this trial Barcaldine gave three stone and nearly half a furlong start to Harkness and the amount of ground he made up when he won this trial had to be seen to be believed. No wonder he strained a muscle. Nevertheless he won the Northumberland Plate by two lengths, ridden by Archer, but the trial finished his racing career and he was then retired to stud.'

George Lambton gives a very different account. He writes that after Barcaldine's victory in the Northumberland Plate, in which race he carried 9 stone 10 lbs, he was put by until the autumn and then readied for the Cambridgeshire in which he was handicapped at 10 stone.

> 'One morning at exercise I met Robert Peck and he said, "I am going to try Barcaldine, come and see it." He was tried with a smart horse in Fulmen, who had won the Lincoln Handicap. Peck told me the weights, which I have forgotten, but he said, "If he can just win this trial, he will win the Cambridgeshire." I can see it now. They were tried up the Cambridgeshire course and at the Red Post Barcaldine, with Archer riding, left the others as though they were rocking horses, and came home alone, except for Robert Peck who was galloping alongside of him on his hack, cheering him on with his hat in his hand like a huntsman with his hounds. Fulmen was second, many lengths in front of the others. It was some trial and Peck was bubbling over, saying there never was such a horse and that the Cambridgeshire was a certainty. Alas, for his hopes, the gallop found out a weak spot, and Barcaldine never ran again.'

At stud Barcaldine achieved success in a career unhappily cut short by an early death from kidney trouble at the age of fifteen, in 1893. His first classic success was with Mimi, who won both the One Thousand Guineas and the Oaks two years before her sire died. In the same year his son, Morion, won the Ascot Gold Cup. Morion was a good racehorse, a powerful 16hh dark bay with black points and, unlike his sire, a beautifully tempered horse. He was slow to mature and ran only once as a two-year-old, scrambling home by a short head from a selling plater at Newmarket. The next season he won the Craven Stakes and the Payne Stakes at Ascot and went on to win the Royal Hunt Cup with 7 stone 9 lbs, the heaviest weight carried successfully by a three-year-old in that race up to that time. He was lucky to win the Bunbury Stakes at Newmarket but had he lost it would have been through no fault of his own. His jockey, George Barrett, thought the winning post was at the top of the rise instead of in the Dip and it was by pure chance that he was lobbing along in front as they passed the winning post. He won the Breeder's St Leger and the Great Foal Stakes. Thus he won seven of his eight races at three, his only defeat was in the Cambridgeshire carrying 8 stone 13 lbs, a big burden for one of his age. The next year Morion won the Ascot Gold Cup. He was first past the post in the Jockey Club Cup, for which he started at 8–1 on. He only just got home by a neck from the only other runner, Patrick Blue, on to whom he had been hanging badly, so it was no surprise when he lost the race on an objection.

When Morion retired to stud a big offer was refused for him to go to Germany but he remained in England to be mated with the cream of the Thoroughbred aristocracy. In spite of the wonderful chances he had, Morion could get nothing of classic standard and the best he got was a useful filly in La Veine and Strongbow, winner of the Ebor Handicap, and he could only do this with the help of the famous mare La Fleche, winner of the fillies' Triple Crown, as both of these came from matings with her. This mare mated to Islinglass, winner of the Triple Crown, bred John o'Gaunt, second in the Derby. This must be the nearest that a winner of the Derby and a winner of the Oaks mated together have got to breeding a Derby winner; and it took two winners of the Triple Crown to do that! It was a pity that the offer made for Morion to go to Germany was refused as, had it not been, one of the tragedies of the 1913 Derby would have been averted, for Morion got Pawky, the dam of Aboyeur.

1913 was a memorable year on the Turf. The Derby-winning favourite was disqualified, a suffragette was killed pulling down the King's horse in the same race, another pulled down Tracery as he was winning the Ascot Gold Cup, two great 'chefs-de-race' appeared – The Tetrarch, in a blaze of glory, and Son in Law, unnoticed. The horse that eventually won the Derby in the inquiry room was Aboyeur, son of Pawky a daughter of Morion. Aboyeur started at 100–1 for the Derby, a price commensurate with his previous form. The favourite, Craganour, was the champion juvenile of his year and thus favourite for the Two Thousand Guineas. Saxby, who rode him in this race, passed the post sitting still and riding with complete confidence. There was a surprise therefore when the verdict went to Louvois racing wide out on the Newmarket course. Saxby was blamed for having thrown the race away, as, had he shaken up Craganour, there is little doubt that he would have won. Most of the onlookers thought he had, including Sydney Galtrey, who adds, however, 'I am not so sure today. I have seen too many optical illusions on the Newmarket course.' A few weeks later Craganour won the Newmarket Stakes three and a half lengths in front of Louvois, who was third.

For some time there was doubt as to who would ride Craganour at Epsom, as the stable had discarded its jockey after he had been beaten on Craganour in the Guineas, and Danny Maher, who had won on the colt in the Newmarket Stakes, had a retainer to ride for Lord Rosebery. As Lord Rosebery's nomination for the Derby was the filly Prue, who only appeared to have a very remote chance, hopes were entertained that Maher might be released from his retainer so that he could ride the favourite. But it was not to be and the connections of Craganour had to look elsewhere. Eventually they brought the American jockey, Johnny Rieff, over from France, which caused considerable umbrage among the available English jockeys.

In the Derby, Aboyeur was the first to break and went on clear of Craganour. As the packed field rounded Tattenham Corner, Miss Emily Davison, a suffragette, rushed among the horses. Walter Earl on Agadir managed to swing his mount clear and round her, but Herbert Jones, on the King's horse Anmer, crashed straight into the woman, who died four days later. Craganour then drew up to Aboyeur in the lead, with Frank Wootton on Shogun trying to find a way through on the fence. Craganour rolled on to Aboyeur, who closed the gap on the rails, causing Wootton to snatch up Shogun and in doing so interfere with Day Comet. Aboyeur then began to hang out badly on to Craganour. Whether he was unbalanced by the bump he had received or whether he had hung in during his previous races, I do not know. It is significant that he was wearing blinkers. In all probability he was tiring, as he had been in front from barrier rise. Aboyeur hanging on to Craganour carried the favourite away from the rails and, in so doing, the pair must have interfered with Louvois and also with Great Sport and Nimbus. The last named had also run into trouble when Anmer had been brought down; if he had had a trouble-free run and won there might have been two Derby winners with the same name! The finish has been generally described as a scrimmaging and bumping one. As they went past the post Craganour had his head in front of Aboyeur, who was hard up against his inside with Louvois, ridden by Saxby, a neck back on Aboyeur's inside.

The number of the favourite went into the frame and for some time there was no hint of an objection, except from Lord Rosebery who remarked, 'If there's an objection the second is sure to get the race.' Then a rumour started that all was not well, so it was with relief that Jack Robinson, trainer of Craganour, heard the 'All right!' shouted. Sidney Galtrey describes the scene:

'Craganour was now being walked towards the gate leading on to the course when there came the sharp order to bring the horse back. "Who," said the voice, "had given the authority for the 'All Right' to be given?" The speaker was Lord Durham, looking rather fierce and terribly serious.'

The stewards had themselves objected.

There were few in the crowd that believed that the race would be taken away from the favourite, but indeed it was, with the announcement:

'The stewards objected to the winner on the grounds that he jostled the second horse. After hearing the evidence of the judge and several of the jockeys riding in the race, they found that Craganour, the winner, did not keep a straight course and interfered with Shogun, Day Comet and Aboyeur. Having bumped and bored the second horse, they disqualified Craganour and awarded the race to Aboyeur.'

Roger Mortimer, in *The History of the Derby Stakes*, writes that

'Lord Rosebery, who had a runner in the race, did not sit on the objection, but he was in the room the whole time and subsequently stated that the evidence was clear and the stewards had no option but to disqualify Craganour.'

Whose evidence? Before discussing the rights or wrongs of the case, it is as well to consider the reliability of the evidence called. As regards the jockeys' evidence, I myself have sat on hundreds of enquiries as a stipendiary steward and as a racemeeting steward and I state emphatically that it is only with the greatest reluctance that I would call a jockey as a witness. It is a waste of time. Sir Gordon Richards, in his autobiography, describes a fracas at the finish of the Cesarewitch in which he was concerned with the lightweight jockey, Johnny Dines.

'We were all summoned into the stewards' room immediately afterwards, but by this time Johnny was just as alarmed about the whole thing as I was. I am afraid that I denied that anything had happened that I knew anything about, and you can be quite sure that, before the stewards, Johnny entirely agreed with me.'

I mention this because years later when Lord Hamilton, Senior Steward of the Jockey Club, retired, he wrote to Fred Darling, leading trainer between the wars, recalling the incident: 'Richards looked straight at me, and I knew he was speaking the truth.'

If such an eminent member of his profession admits this, what of the others? Apart from the evidence in general given by jockeys, here are Steve Donoghue's comments on the evidence given at this particular objection:

'Saxby's evidence was taken by the stewards. How could it have been unprejudiced after – to say the least – the unfortunate way the jockey had been treated by the connections of Craganour? Jockeys are, like other people, only human, and here was a golden opportunity for anyone to get his own back.'

Apart from his revenge the disqualification of the winner would have meant Saxby's mount being moved up from third to second. Apart from Saxby, other jockeys resented the engagement of an American jockey from abroad to ride the favourite. So much for the value of evidence given by jockeys. What of that of the judge? Mr Robinson, looking down the course, had seen Craganour roll into and bump Aboyeur. But had he seen the retaliation by Aboyeur hanging out from the rail on to Craganour and carrying him out. The probability is not, for the judge's eyes must leave the horses as they get close home and line up on the winning post.

There was no doubt that Craganour did bump Aboyeur and it is possible that this was the reason that Aboyeur began to hang. Up to this point, Craganour was to blame, but when Aboyeur began to hang, did his rider take any steps to remedy the matter? Apparently not. The photographs of the finish confirm this. Piper, on Aboyeur, can be plainly seen with his whip held out in his left hand, not only making no attempt to keep his mount off the favourite, but actually causing him to run away from the whip into Craganour. Why did Piper not object? Probably because he knew that he was far from guiltless. It is hard to believe that he would not have objected if he thought he had a case

Why did the stewards object? Did they all watch the race from the same position? Why the delay in laying an objection? Did they discuss the matter among their number, one of whom was Lord Rosebery, who did not sit, but who had already expressed his opinion?

Bower Ismay, owner of Craganour, lodged an appeal, but this was disallowed because it was not lodged within the allotted time. Disbarred from appealing, Ismay got an injunction from the courts to restrain the stakeholders from paying out. In the meantime a big offer for Craganour came from the Argentine so Ismay, who had lost the Guineas through his jockey and the Derby on an objection, decided to let the colt go, accepted the offer and withdrew the court case.

Aboyeur ran twice more finishing third in the St George Stakes at Liverpool, and second in the Gordon Stakes at Goodwood before being sold to Russia for a fifth of the price given for Craganour. Louvois won the Prince of Wales's Stakes at Royal Ascot and finished second to Tracery in the Eclipse. Whether he or Shogun or Nimbus would have beaten Craganour with a clear run we shall, of course, never know. Richard Marsh, the King's trainer, says, 'I will always maintain that it was a tragic decision which was not merited.' Jack Jarvis, who watched the race from the top of the stands, not unnaturally agreed with his patron Lord Rosebery, and told me that he was a supporter of Aboyeur's claim to the race.

Winkfield was not a bit like his full brother Morion; he was a chestnut not a bay and was a sprinter (and a very moderate one at that) not a stayer. According to Richard Marsh he won a selling race at Liverpool and was sold to a vet in Swindon. After the vet's death, he found his way to Ireland, where, surprising as it may seem, he became the sire of the good stayer Bachelor's Button, famous as the horse that beat the great Pretty Polly in the Ascot Gold Cup in 1906. The defeat of this darling of the public had been prophesied by Danny Maher, who did not think she was a true stayer. He had ridden the filly in the Prix du Conseil Municipal, which was run in fast time and in very heavy going and, although she started at odds of 2–1 on, she had not really seen it out and was beaten two and a half lengths. In a field of four in the Jockey Club Cup Pretty Polly and Bachelor's Button, with Maher up, drew well clear of the others and the filly won by half a length. Despite this Maher maintained he was right and said that if he had another one to go along with them he would have outstayed the filly. 'If they meet in the Ascot Gold Cup next year, Bachelor's Button will win,' he declared. They did meet, and the general opinion was that Pretty Polly was a certainty and she started at long odds-on. But the many were wrong and Maher was right, for Pretty Polly failed to see out the two and a half miles of the testing Ascot course and Bachelor's Button beat her. Danny Maher must have known the capabilities of the Gold Cup winner well, for when he was riding a horse of Lord Derby's, His Majesty, in receipt of 11 lbs from Bachelor's Button, who was looked upon as a good thing, he stated emphatically that the son of Winkfield would not act on the cramped Stockton course. Again he was right, and he won on His Majesty, Bachelor's Button no better than fourth. In all, Bachelor's Button won sixteen races. It may have seemed surprising that Winkfield should sire such a splendid stayer, but this ability of horses that do not themselves stay to get horses that do stay is not uncommon providing they themselves have a pedigree of stamina. Desmond, sire of the Derby pair Craganour and Aboyeur, and Sundridge, sire of the Derby winner Sunstar, are other examples of this around that time.

Another well-known son of Winkfield, Winkfield's Pride, won both the Cambridgeshire and the Lincoln, both important races in those days. He was one of the most famous of handicappers, although not quite of classic standard and he was easily beaten by Persimmon in the Ascot Gold Cup. However, he won the Doncaster Cup and was successful both on the racecourse and at stud in France, where he won the Prix du Conseil Municipal and sired the French Derby winner, Finnasseur.

Sir Visto credited his sire, Barcaldine, with the Derby and won both that classic and the St Leger in what has been put down as a moderate year. He had run third in both the Two Thousand Guineas and the Newmarket Stakes before the Derby and started at 9–1 in what was an open betting race. Two furlongs out, it was Curzon, a rank outsider (and a gelding at that!) who looked like winning but Sam Loates brought Sir Visto with a well-timed run to beat Curzon by threequarters of a length. Before the St Leger rumours were that the Derby winner had been injured in his box and was a doubtful runner. He had met with an accident but it was of no consequence and he started favourite for the last classic at 9–4. It was a desperate race all the way up the straight, between Sir Visto and Washington Singer's Telescope. The former got the better of it, with the third distanced behind them. Sir Visto went to stand at Mentmore, the stud of his owner, Lord Rosebery, but had no success and was downgraded and sent to Ireland.

Besides Winkfield there was another moderate son of Barcaldine's whose descendants rose to stardom. Goodfellow was a very moderate horse whose only win was in a maiden plate on the old Harpenden course. Goodfellow had a son called Chaleureux, who was bred by Lady Stamford. He was bought out of a selling race by the Newmarket trainer George Blackwell, who brought off a big coup with him in the Cesarewitch in 1898, after which Chaleureux went on to win the Manchester November Handicap. Racing in the first half of this century was one of the passports to social recognition and the key to the Royal Enclosure, if not to the Jockey Club itself. Fortunes found in the blue clay of Kimberley were lavishly spent on the green grass of Ascot and Newmarket. From the classic-winning owners who made up this background, the Chevalier Ginistrelli – the owner, breeder and trainer of Signorina – stands out, rather pathetic yet splendid, like Strube's little man, his classic victories the triumph of a lover of horses over those with unlimited bank balances. His was not the success of a businessman instructing his trainer to buy a dozen yearlings regardless of cost; his was the reward, too often denied, of a man who bred, trained and raced his own horses. The Chevalier Ginistrelli arrived from Italy with a small string of horses and set up at Newmarket, where he was thought of as something of a misfit. In fact, to anyone who loved horses and racing as much as he did, it must have been a spiritual home and an earthly paradise. Richard Marsh gives him his due when he writes,

'I had much respect for the old Italian sportsman, who bred and owned the filly. That he loved her as he would a child of his own goes without saying. After all he did a wonderful thing in training.'

The humble stable of the Chevalier first caught the public eye with the wonderful two-year-old career of Signorina, when this filly ran up a record of nine victories without defeat. Sir George Chetwynd describes her 'as the beautiful Signorina' and writes that as a two-year-old she was 'a ready-made racehorse'. She failed to train on, though next season she did win one useful race, but her great record as a juvenile promised great things at stud. She foaled Signorinetta when she was eighteen years old, before that her best produce had been Signorino, who had been third in the Derby to Cicero and Jardy. Chaleureux, at exercise, was led past the paddock in which Signorina was grazing. He neighed and she replied, the Chevalier maintained that the stallion and mare had fallen in love. The result of the subsequent mating was Signorinetta.

As a two-year-old Signorinetta was nothing out of the ordinary, running six times and winning her last race. Before the Derby, she ran unplaced in the One Thousand Guineas and the Newmarket Stakes, so that her chances at Epsom appeared very remote, 100–1 in fact. Her owner, however, fancied her and backed her, encouraging his friends to do likewise. He felt certain she would stay and worked her accordingly. He was right: she did stay and the rest didn't. Beautifully ridden by Billie Bullock, she cruised past the leaders to win easily. The stunned silence which greeted her was lengthened by not one of the six most fancied horses finishing in the first three.

Her owner had seen his faith fulfilled and he proudly led his heroine in. Two days after, the great triumph was repeated when Signorinetta dealt with the Oaks field, depleted by the fall of the Guineas winner Rhodora, in just as easy a fashion. And so Chevalier Ginistrelli's cup of joy was filled. As Vincent Orchard writes, 'Oaks day must have been a red letter day for the proud Chevalier. After Signorinetta's rider had weighed in, King Edward VII sent for her owner, congratulated him, and then took him by the arm and, as it were, showed him to the wildly cheering crowd.'

A daughter of Barcaldine named Barley went to Australia, where she bred Malster, winner of many races including the AJC Derby and the VTC Derby and was champion sire three years in succession from 1910–1912 and again in 1915.

The son of Barcaldine to hand on the Matchem line was Marco.

CHAPTER 6

OVER THE STICKS

Marco was not a classic winner, but the American writer A. E. T. Watson writes that he was probably the best three-year-old of 1895, when the very moderate Sir Visto beat a half-bred gelding in the Derby. He proved a good horse at stud and, so great an influence did he have on steeplechasers, that the possession of a strain of Marco is almost essential on a passport for entry into the winner's enclosure at Aintree or Cheltenham. He was a chestnut with a blaze and two hind stockings. He inherited the strong shoulders of his sire, but, from his photograph, appears very light in the gaskins for such a strongly made horse. He is said to have had defective forelegs but, in spite of this handicap, he was able to do his fair share of racing. As a two-year-old he won three of his five races. At three, he won five races including the Cambridge-shire by three lengths. Although Marco raced for two more seasons, he was not so successful as he had been at three years old, running eleven times for two wins. From this form he could not expect to get the best of mares when he went to stud, neverthe-less, when given the opportunity, he proved himself capable of getting a horse of classic stature and from the good mare Chelan-dry he bred a winner of the Two Thousand Guineas.

Neil Gow, owned and bred by Lord Rosebery, the former Prime Minister, was a chestnut horse, full of quality and deserving the epithet 'beautiful'. His only fault was his hocks and they proved his undoing in his preparation for the Derby, but apart from that he was the most inspiring specimen of a Thoroughbred. He was a horse with a mind of his own and was as bad-tempered as his grandfather had been, being very troublesome at the gate, which trait cost him his first two races. From then on he turned out a brilliant two-year-old, winning the National Breeders' Produce Stakes by four lengths, the Prince of Wales Stakes at Goodwood by six lengths, the Champagne Stakes, beating the odds-on favourite Lemberg, and the Imperial Produce Stakes by a head. Lemberg was unbeaten at the time he met Neil Gow, having previously won the New Stakes at Ascot by four lengths, the Chesterfield Stakes, and the Rous Memorial at Goodwood. Lemberg continued his winning ways by scoring another Rous Memorial at Newmarket, the Middle Park Plate in which he beat the American colt Whisk Broom by a neck, a distance which he extended to five lengths in the Dewhurst Plate.

Thus the stage was set for what promised to be a great struggle between two brilliant colts for the next year's classics. This was a vintage year for, besides these two, the three-year-olds of 1910 were of high quality. Whisk Broom, mentioned above, was a great success in his own country, there was a great horse to appear in the St Leger winner Swynford, and, when Neil Gow went wrong for the Derby, there was game little Greenback to take his place and make a great race of it with Lemberg. Neil Gow made his first appearance of the season when winning the Craven Stakes and he then met Lemberg, who was making his in the Two Thousand Guineas. George Lambton writes,

'I went some way down the course to see the race and it was indeed one worth seeing. Coming into the Dip, Lemberg, who was ridden by Dillon, and Neil Gow were close together on the Stand side, and, after Whisk Broom had made a bold show, they singled themselves out from the rest of the field, Lemberg with a trifling advantage. Then Danny sat down to ride with that confidence and determination that will not be beaten. Leaning over the rails close to the struggling pair I could see the jockeys' desperate faces, the horses with their ears flat back on their heads, both running as true as steel; it was a great sight.'

And it was a great race, just on the post Danny Maher inched Neil Gow up to win by a short head.

George Lambton does not tell of the part that his brother, Lord Durham, was to play. Lord Durham objected strongly to the clamour of the rooks in the elms at Harraton House, where Neil Gow was trained. His trainer, Percy Peck, believed that the rooks in the elms had the same powers as the monkeys on the Rock of Gibraltar and the ravens in the Tower of London, and, when, he heard that an eviction order was to be served on them, he was filled with foreboding. He was right, for on the very day that sentence was carried out on the rookery, Neil Gow threw a curb. While Lemberg was winning his Derby trial Neil Gow was confined to walking exercise. The two colts were the only ones that had been seriously backed for the Derby that year so, in view of Neil Gow's set-back, Lemberg started favourite. Greenback made the running until two furlongs out, where Dillon shot Lemberg into the lead and it looked all over, but Greenback gamely struggled back and the favourite hung on to win by only a neck, with Neil Gow fourth. At Sandown, the Derby and Guineas winners met again in the Eclipse Stakes and a terrific race resulted, the judge being unable to separate them at the finish. It says a lot for the genuineness of these two colts that they could reproduce their running in the Guineas almost to an ounce. The hard struggle on hard going had knocked up Neil Gow and he never ran again.

Another good son of Marco was Beppo, who won the Jockey Club Stakes and the Hardwicke Stakes and was the sire of the Oaks winner, My Dear, whose dam was a half sister of Lemberg, Neil Gow's rival. She was sexually amiss in the One Thousand Guineas, which was won by Lord Derby's Ferry at 50–1 in a small field. Ferry was to have missed the Oaks as the stable thought they had a better one in Stony Ford, but, shortly before the race, the latter hit herself in a gallop so it was decided to start both fillies. Skeets Martin had the ride on Stony Ford, while Steve Donoghue rode My Dear, who started favourite. Stony Ford appeared to have the Oaks well in hand when, for some reason or another, she started to veer over and crossed My Dear. At the subsequent objection she was disqualified as, apart from the crossing, My Dear had also apparently received a bump from Stony Ford further down the course. In the St Leger, My Dear ran up against the great Gainsborough to whom she ran second.

At stud she, unfortunately only produced colts so we have no line coming down from her.

Beppo also got Aleppo. He was out of a half sister to Lemberg's dam. Aleppo got beaten by a neck in the Goodwood Cup in 1913, and his owner was not in the best of moods when approached by an agent to sell his horse for export as he remarked, 'I'm not sure whether I want to sell him or geld him.' Luckily he did neither and Aleppo won the next year's Ascot Gold Cup.

Beppo headed the list of broodmare sires at the very early age of fourteen. He was assisted in this by the lack of racing during the Great War and by the progeny of one mare, his daughter Gay Laura, who produced the winner of the Triple Crown. Gay Crusader did not impress his trainer, Alec Taylor, on his arrival in his yard as a yearling. He was on the small side, mean-looking and light. In his first trial he ran a dead-heat with Aleli at level weights. He then got sore shins and was put away till the backend, when he was tried again with Aleli whom he beat by six lengths. As a three-year-old he ran second first time out with Aleli, now in receipt of 18 lbs, a length away third. He was obviously coming on all the time. Alec Taylor had another runner in the Two Thousand Guineas besides Gay Crusader. This was Lord Astor's Magpie. Through Aleli, Alec Taylor knew there was not much between the two colts and he did not know which was going to win, although he was confident of running first and second. From barrier rise the pair drew away from the field and raced neck and neck all the way. Magpie was a lazy horse, who would do no more than he need and, although Gay Crusader was running a great race and responding to Donoghue's urgings, Magpie was going every bit as well and it seemed likely that in response to the whip he might draw out a little more. Steve Donoghue kept his mount close up to Otto Madden's whip hand. The veteran jockey had only returned to the saddle due to the shortage of jockeys during the Great War, and his reactions were not as quick as they had been; they were past the post before he could change his whip, with Gay Crusader a head to the good. Steve Donoghue states that he was very lucky to beat Magpie that day. The two never met again as Magpie was sold to Australia, where he made a great name for himself as a sire and as a sire of broodmares.

When Gay Crusader stripped for the Derby, his improved appearance amazed the critics: he was now a beautiful horse. As Sidney Galtrey writes, 'There was nothing superfluous about him, neither flesh nor bone. He was the absolute racing machine,' and Vincent Orchard writes, 'he looked magnificent and was a perfectly trained specimen of the Thoroughbred.' The latter goes on to write of the Derby that Donoghue rode an odd sort of race on him, trying on three occasions to pass Dark Legend on the inside to secure the rails position. Gay Crusader must have lost several lengths in the process, but it made not the slightest difference when his rider began his run; the race was over a long way before the winning post was reached.

Probably, Donoghue's riding tactics were designed to counteract what he describes as the horse's high spirits, for Gay Crusader was liable to duck and shy from patches or shadows. Donoghue adopted some unorthodox methods when riding him: on one occasion, lacking a pacemaker, he gave another horse a whack over the hindquarters. After the Derby, Gay Crusader proved invincible. He won the St Leger by six lengths, the Gold Cup (run at Newmarket because of the war) at 100–8 on by fifteen lengths, and his other two races that season just as easily. He went into training the next season with the Gold Cup as his objective. With Donoghue up, he was given a full-scale work-out and galloped magnificently; then the blow fell, he had strained a tendon. How good was Gay Crusader? Alec Taylor gave a carefully expressed opinion that he was the best horse he ever trained. Steve Donoghue stated, 'I consider Gay Crusader to be the best racehorse I ever rode.' Considering the number of top-class racehorses with whom these two were associated, it places Gay Crusader very high in the Thoroughbred world. At stud, he started with all the wonderful chances a Triple Crown winner would expect; they didn't get him very far. His stock got the reputation of not being genuine, and there was a look of white in their eye that trainers disliked. He failed to get a classic winner.

Marco's next best to Neil Gow was Omar Khayam. He appeared during the war years and was sold for 300 guineas as a yearling and proved a wonderful bargain. He was a chestnut, whose beauty has been described as 'exquisite' – he had rather a feminine neck

F. C. Turner's highly imaginative depiction of Sham, the Godolphin Arabian, dated 1845.

ABOVE: Stubbs' engraving of the Godolphin Arabian. *(Courtesy the Trustees of the British Museum)*

RIGHT: A painting by an unknown artist, of the second Lord Godolphin, after whom the Arabian was named. *(Courtesy The European Racehorse)*

Harry Hall's painting of Blink Bonny (by Melbourne out of Queen Mary).
(Courtesy Arthur Ackermann & Son Ltd)

One of Blink Bonny's famous sons, Blair Athol.

West Australian with Frank Buckle up, painted by Henry Alken Junior (1810–1894)
(Courtesy Arthur Ackermann & Son Ltd)

A beautiful portrait of the classic winner, Rockingham,
by John Ferneley Senior.

The American-bred Iroquois, a great-grandson of West Australian,
who crossed the Atlantic to win the Derby of 1881,
ridden by Fred Archer.

Marco, a son of Barcaldine, who handed on the Matchem line. The American writer A. E. T. Watson described him as probably the best three-year-old of 1895. *(Courtesy The European Racehorse)*

Marco's son, Marcovil, a strongly made chestnut of quality with a blaze. *(Courtesy The European Racehorse)*

Marcovil's son, Hurry On – nothing ever got close enough to Hurry On to give any idea of his capabilities, and there was no doubt about his stamina. *(Courtesy The European Racehorse)*

Hurry On's second Derby winner, Coronach – a big, impressive chestnut horse with a white face. *(Courtesy The European Racehorse)*

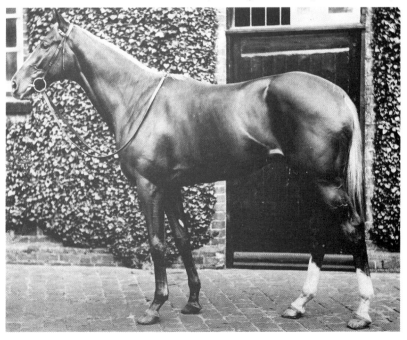

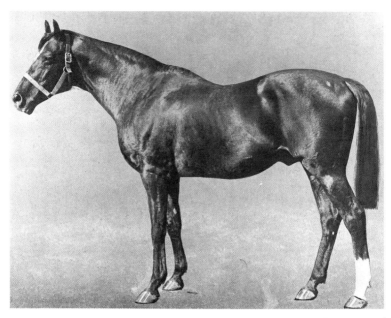

Montrose, one of Coronach's sons, was a useful but not brilliant racehorse. He was not patronised by the best in his own country but his stock had only to put their feet on South African soil to start winning races over there.

Relic, the son of War Relic who revitalised the Matchem line in Europe just after the Second World War.
(Courtesy The European Racehorse)

and head. He was the best of his classic year. In 1917 he became the first imported horse to win the Kentucky Derby and won thirteen races including the Saratoga Cup, the Dwyer, the Travers and the Realization Stakes. He was a prolific sire.

With the descendants of Marco, the story of the Matchem line turns for a while from summer green turf to mud-sodden courses under leaden skies, where the so-called humbler relations of the classic winners send the gorse tops flying. Whatever the appeal of Ascot or Epsom, to the lover of horses, to the true horseman, the Grand National stands alone. When the field thunders into the first fence at Aintree, late at night there is a tensing of muscles in Australia, on the racecourses of South Africa there is an intake of breath, from Melbourne to Maryland this moment is the climax of the horseman's year.

The descendants of the Godolphin Arabian were far from unknown over fences before Marco. The 'jumping blood' of Melbourne had long been famous and it is probable that his sire, Humphrey Clinker, had an even greater influence on steeplechasers than did Melbourne as Lord FitzWilliam sent his horse to stand in Ireland for the benefit of his Wicklow tenants. When he returned to England, Humphrey Clinker left a large tribe behind him; many cases of half-bred doubtless trace to him. The great chaser Cloister, who won the Grand National carrying 12 stone 7 lbs, was by Ascetic, a grandson of Melbourne. In this century there has been a great resurgence of the 'jumping blood', for between the wars the greatest sire of chasers was My Prince who was by Marco's son, Marcovil, who was succeeded by Cottage, who was out of a daughter of Marco.

The first of Marco's line to win the Grand National was the chestnut Sprig, by Marco himself. There was a sad romance about his victory. His breeder, Richard Partridge, a captain in the Shropshire Yeomanry, had been killed in action a few weeks before the armistice, and his mother, faithful to a promise, had put Sprig in training, hoping to realise her son's ambition to win the great race. Sprig, when he won, was no stranger to Aintree, for he had completed the course twice previously to finish fourth in the Grand National. In 1927, ridden by Ted Leader, he carried

12 stone 4 lbs and started favourite for the second time. In view of his previous performances no doubts were entertained about Sprig's ability to jump the Aintree course, and, as he took them away into the country for the second time a popular victory seemed assured; but, when a loose horse ran across him going into Becher's Brook, disaster nearly overtook him. Sprig got over somehow, but he pecked badly and lost his position at the head of the field. At the Canal Turn he made a most spectacular jump, taking off fifth and landing in front. The favourite turned for home in the lead, while behind him Jack Anthony was gradually bringing Brights Boy up and these two good chasers jumped the last fence together. Ted Leader and Jack Anthony were both hard at work when the one-eyed hunter, Bovril III, ridden by his owner delivered a strong challenge. Very tired, Sprig hung on gamely to beat Bovril III a length with Brights Boy third.

The next two years where those in which the famous Easter Hero performed, the first a fiasco, the second a gallant defeat. Easter Hero was a son of My Prince, a magnificent horse in looks and great in deeds. He was a headstrong horse, a fast impetuous jumper and, in his first season, he fell three times in Ireland although coming to England to win at Manchester. The next season he visited England to win three races off the reel before returning to Ireland in the summer of 1927. In the November of that year he was back again to win the Becher Chase at Aintree and followed this up with two victories at Kempton. He made his first appearance in the Grand National in the colours of the millionaire financier, Captain Loewenstein, who had bought him. Easter Hero's part in the Grand National was inglorious indeed, for, not only did he get stuck on top of the fence at the Canal Turn but, in so doing, caused innumerable horses to refuse, which eventually led to Tipperary Tim being the only one not to fall and coming home at a 100-1. Captain Loewenstein mysteriously disappeared from an aeroplane over the English Channel and Easter Hero was bought by J. H. Whitney, who sent him to be trained by Jack Anthony. When he appeared the next season, the big chestnut had put on weight and seemed less impetuous. At the start of the season he was kept to hurdling, at which game he proved himself about the best in the country, winning four races in succession. He returned to chasing with a fluent win in the Cheltenham Gold Cup, which he won by twenty lengths.

It was not surprising that he carried top weight in the Grand National and that he was favourite at 9–2, a short price in view of the enormous field of sixty-six, for Tipperary Tim's surprising victory had filled many owners with optimism and encouraged them to run their no-hopers on the off-chance. Shouldering his burden in grand style, Easter Hero led throughout the first circuit and was still in front when they came to the Canal Turn, here he was joined by Richmond II and Sandy Hook. They rose as one and the three jockeys were knee to knee as they landed. Sandy Hook fell at the fence after Valentine's and here Easter Hero spread a plate. Soon after, Richmond II dropped back exhausted, but the locked battle had left its mark on the favourite and gallantly as he struggled, he had not enough left in reserve to withstand the challenge of another son of My Prince, Gregalach. Easter Hero, had he not spread a plate, might well have achieved what with hindsight seems the impossible, to give 17 lbs to Gregalach over the National course. How hard a task this was Gregalach showed two years later when, shouldering 12 stone, Gregalach finished second within a length and a half of Grakle.

The next season Easter Hero appeared only three times to win on each occasion, the last being the Cheltenham Gold Cup. The very fast Gib was fancied to beat the champion and was upsides with him when he fell, leaving Easter Hero to canter home twenty lengths in front of Grakle. The following season was his last. He opened it by frightening away the opposition and walking over for the Penkridge Chase at Wolverhampton. Then, after winning at Leicester and Sandown at odds of 6–1 on, he was beaten a head trying to give 25 lbs to Desert Chief at Lingfield. He came to Aintree once more; again he was top weight and again he was favourite. At Becher's Brook the second time round he was going well and in the race with a great chance, when Solanum fell right in his path. Easter Hero made a gallant attempt to avoid the fallen horse; he dodged to the left and back to the right and in so doing unseated Fred Rees and galloped on riderless. The next day he came out for the Champion Chase and, after pecking at the last fence, got up to force a dead-heat. This was his farewell appearance. Easter Hero was a hero indeed. In England he won eighteen races, only meeting defeat once, and then only by a head, other than in his first season and in the National. His finest race might well have been his second to Gregalach in the Grand National.

Reynoldstown, another son of My Prince, won the Grand National twice, the only horse to achieve this feat since Manifesto at the end of the last century. Reynoldstown was a dark brown, almost black horse, named after his birthplace in County Kildare. His victory at seven years old, on the occasion of his first win, was a family affair, as he was owned and trained by Major Noel Furlong and ridden by his son Frank. He was opposed by that famous chaser Golden Miller, who in the previous year had achieved the hitherto unaccomplished feat of winning the double of the Cheltenham Gold Cup and the Grand National in the same year, and by the stout-hearted little Thomond II, third to 'the Miller' in the previous National. These two had just taken part in a memorable duel for the Cheltenham Gold Cup, in which, after one of the greatest steeplechases ever seen, Dorothy Paget's Golden Miller had beaten Thomond II, racing in the well-known Whitney colours, which had also been carried by Easter Hero. Golden Miller was made favourite to repeat the Cup/National double, but he appeared to have broken down when he refused at Valentine's and unseated his jockey. At Becher's Brook the second time round, Thomond II bumped Reynoldstown but, as might be expected of one his diminutive size, came off worst. Despite this he came on in the lead and jumped the Canal Turn clear of Reynoldstown. As they came on to the racecourse Reynoldstown passed Thomond II, but the little chestnut battled on and drew up to Reynoldstown at the last fence. The two rose together but Thomond II jumped to the right and they collided on landing, but again Reynoldstown recovered first and carried on up the straight to win in record time.

Reynoldstown maintained his form between his two Nationals and was allotted 12 stone 2 lbs, Golden Miller once again being at the top of the handicap. The race was dominated by the sparkling display of the 100–1 outsider, Davy Jones, who took up the running at Valentine's first time round, jumping fence after fence magnificently. Going away from the stands on the second circuit

Reynoldstown set off after the flying Davy Jones and the pair were twenty lengths clear of the field at Becher's Brook. At the last fence before coming on to the racecourse, Reynoldstown received interference from a loose horse and blundered badly. From the stands it seemed he must fall but Fulke Walwyn, by some miracle, got back into the saddle, and set off to try and catch Davy Jones, who was racing away some twenty lengths in front. It appeared at that moment that nothing could prevent Anthony Mildmay on Davy Jones from winning the National. We could not foresee the future, to know what was to befall such as Zahia and Devon Loch, or to guess that Fate, unable to control her meddling fingers, was to play the first of her three cruel tricks at Aintree. Coming to the last fence the leader veered off to the left, and, with broken reins dangling, galloped off the course. Reynoldstown jumped the last fence and came up the straight well clear of Harry 'Foxhunter' Llewellyn on the one-paced but faultless jumper Ego, and the two 'Princes', Bachelor Prince and Crown Prince. Had Davy Jones kept his course it would have been an all-amateur Grand National. As it was, Fulke Walwyn, Ronnie Strutt and Harry Llewellyn finished in the first four.

My Prince did not have to wait long before he sired another National winner, for the very next year, the race was won by his son, Royal Mail. He was a black horse owned by his amateur rider Lloyd Thomas and trained by Ivor Anthony, and was eight years old when he won his National. Royal Mail had run consistently through the season. In receipt of 11 lbs he had beaten Golden Miller at Aintree in November and in the National he was getting 8 lbs with 'The Miller' once more top weight, the latter starting favourite. Golden Miller refused again this year, and, after the mare Pucka Belle had led them past the stands, Royal Mail took up the running and was never headed.

Another son of My Prince, Prince Regent, might well have won a National had not the Second World War years coincided with his peak. Prince Regent was bought at Ballsbridge by J. V. Rank as a yearling for 320 guineas. He made up into a fine, deep-hearted, muscular bay standing 16.3 hh. Although he had won a few races previously, Prince Regent did not really show his true qualities until he was seven years old. At that age he won in a

canter by twenty lengths at Naas, carried 12 stone 7 lbs to win by
four lengths at Navan, and beat Pulcher at Baldoyle giving him
nearly 2 stone. These fluent victories earned 'The Prince' top
weight in the Irish Grand National, which he won by a length
from Golden Jack. From then on his battle was with the
handicapper. Rarely asked to concede less than 3 stone or so to
his opponents, his number was continually in the frame over three
seasons, either in first or second place.

At last the war was over, so with steeplechasing resumed in
their own country, English racegoers, starved for so long of an
Easter Hero or a Golden Miller, had once again the chance to
see a champion chaser. Prince Regent's first appearance in
England was in his owner's home county and he won at Wetherby
easily at 10–1 on. As was expected Prince Regent proved himself
a worthy champion at Cheltenham, where he easily won the Gold
Cup. Now came Prince Regent's first chance to win a Grand
National. He was allotted top weight and installed as a short-
priced favourite. Although on form it seemed impossible to look
for the winner beyond the Irish champion, there were those, of
whom I was one, who had their doubts. Prince Regent's maternal
grandam was Capdane, a full sister of the flying Diomedes, who
won so many sprint races for Sidney Beer, conductor of the
London Philharmonic Orchestra. 'The Prince' had won many
races over three and a half miles, but was this the right blood to
enable a horse to see out a mile further over the Aintree course,
under a burden of more than 12 stone? One would not think so,
and his National performances, albeit they were in the evening of
his years, would seem to endorse this opinion. In 1946 he ran a
great race up to a point, and that point was two or three fences
from home when he began to tire badly, eventually finishing third
to Lovely Cottage and the fast finishing Jack Finlay, both of whom
of course were receiving a deal of weight. It transpired that Prince
Regent had suffered badly from the attentions of two loose horses
and that Hyde had been forced to use 'The Prince's' speed to
shake them off, and had to go up to the front rank too soon.

The next season Prince Regent started by winning at Leopardstown with Caughoo, who was later to win the National, behind
him. He returned to England to win the Champion Chase at

Aintree by a distance at 6–1 on. Then from the middle of January until a few days after the abandoned Cheltenham meeting a severe frost gripped the land. There was no chance for new stars to rise and once more Prince Regent was top weight for the Grand National and once more he was favourite. As far as his part in the great race was concerned, it was very much a repetition of the previous year. John Hislop, who rode Kami, wrote,

'As we crossed the road with only two more fences to jump I could see Prince Regent in front of me, visibly tiring and still a good way ahead. . . . Coming into the last fence but one there were two loose horses in front of me and, on the inside, Prince Regent. I realised I had no hope of winning, as Kami was tiring; the heavy going had taken toll of his delicate frame, and only his courage and his innate stamina kept him going. But he jumped the fence perfectly, and went on towards the last with, I think, Prince Regent about level with us, but very tired. We landed safely with the long stretch to the winning post spread out in front of us, both tired, but with Prince Regent beaten for sure. I got out my whip and kept swinging it without ever hitting Kami, and he answered nobly, gradually overhauling Mr Rank's gallant horse to take us into third place.'

Prince Regent finished fourth a long way behind Caughoo, whom he had easily beaten at Leopardstown. The next season he was back in November to win the Becher Chase at Aintree at 5–2 on and once more he had top weight in the Grand National but with 12 stone 2 lbs instead of the maximum weight. It seemed that the march of time had caught up with him, as he was already a spent force when carried out at Valentine's. The correspondent of the *Irish Horse* wrote, 'This great chaser, and "great" he had been, was foaled out of his time for the Grand National was not being run in the years when he was at his peak.' Whether he would have won a National is a matter for conjecture – he had speed and courage and could stay within reason, but there is a doubt as to whether he possessed that 'innate stamina' bred in him. He and Easter Hero go down to history as two of the greatest chasers not to have won the Grand National.

Marco's daughter Casetta was put to Tracery. This was the blend of Rock Sand blood with that of West Australian that had proved so successful in America. The result of this mating was Cottage. Although he was bred by Baron Edouard de Rothschild he was trained in England but did not run until he was four years old, his only success in thirteen outings being in the Fitzwilliam Stakes at Doncaster. He went to stand in County Fermoy. The first of his Grand National winners was Workman, who had finished third to Battleship, a scion of the American line of Matchem, and Royal Danieli. Dorothy Paget had bought a brilliant young ex-showjumper, Kilstar, to replace the now aging Golden Miller. Great things were expected of him, but in the National he blundered badly at Becher's the first time round, losing some twenty lengths. Royal Mail, the hero two years previously, was again in the field, but with top weight, and so was Royal Danieli. Royal Mail got round safely but Royal Danieli, a free runner out in front, fell. Workman, well ridden by Tim Hyde, jumped the last in front and ran on to beat the Scottish trained MacMoffat and Kilstar.

The following year, 1940, the Grand National again fell to a descendant of Marco, Lord Stalbridge's Bogskar by Werwolf, by Hurry On, by Marcovil. Werwolf was an outstanding sire of steeplechasers and his son, Bogskar, had been showing great promise in what was to be the last jumping season in England for many years. He was ridden by Flight Sergeant Mervyn Jones, who was later killed in the war that had already broken out at the time of his victory. MacMoffat jumped the water clear of Golden Arrow and Royal Danieli, the three well clear of a strung-out field. Bogskar gradually made progress but even at Valentine's was some twenty lengths behind MacMoffat, who was racing alongside the riderless National Night, also a son of Werwolf. Alder on MacMoffat had to push his mount along, desperately trying to be quit of the loose horse and had no chance to give MacMoffat a breather. Bogskar was coming on relentlessly and the three horses took the last fence together. Macmoffat, jumping slightly left away from the riderless National Night, slightly hampered Bogskar, who pecked but recovered and the Scottish hunter had to be content with second place once again.

There were no more Grand Nationals to be won until 1946 when Lovely Cottage won. It was the year when all eyes were fixed on Prince Regent and that fine chaser's first chance to win the National. The champion did not truly stay and Lovely Cottage took the lead off him at the last fence and ran clean away on the flat. Lovely Cottage, who was nine years old when he won, was bred in County Cork by Mr and Mrs Hyde and was brought up almost as a household pet. A Yorkshire trainer, hearing the horse was for sale, travelled over to look at him and, determined not be done down by the wily Irish, decided to stick to milk when offered more potent refreshment by the hospitable Hydes. The negotiations were prolonged and he had consumed five glasses of milk when he finally stuck his toes in when only £100 apart. 'If only,' he said afterward, 'I had had five glasses of something else my courage wouldn't have failed me! I would have bought the horse and won the Grand National.'

One who affected an unlucky deal was Sir Hervey Bruce, later a trainer in South Africa, who sold the mare, Sheila's Cottage, a few weeks before the Grand National. Sheila's Cottage was by Cottage out of Sheila, who was a granddaughter of Marco's son, Beppo, so the National winner had another strain of the 'jumping blood'. Passing the stands the three leaders over the water were all by Cottage; first over was the good mare Zahia, then Dorothy Paget's Happy Home, with Sheila's Cottage next. Zahia continued to run a great race and nearing home appeared to have the race in safe keeping, when his rider headed on to the National course instead of up to the last fence and the finish. John Hislop, who had fallen on the first circuit on Cloncarrig, was watching from where the horses come on to the racecourse. He writes,

'Zahia was on the inside with First of the Dandies slightly in front, and Sheila's Cottage and Cromwell on their heels. To our dismay, Zahia's rider made for the course which leads to the Chair fence. We shouted and waved at him, but could not attract his attention and before he realised his mistake he had run out.'

Thus occurred the second leg treble with Davy Jones and Devon Loch. With the unlucky Zahia gone, First of the Dandies jumped the last fence in front but was immediately tackled by Sheila's Cottage. A great struggle ensued and the indomitable mare would not give in and with great courage eventually ran First of the Dandies out of it by a length.

There is little doubt that had not the war years intervened, Cottage, who died of a twisted gut in 1942, would have sired even more winners of the Grand National than he did, and we must not leave him without mentioning his brilliant son, Cottage Rake, who won the Cheltenham Gold Cup on three occasions. His first success was in 1948 when his great rival, Cool Customer, fell at the first fence, and his chief opponent turned out to be another son of Cottage in Happy Home. The *Irish Horse* writes,

'The Gold Cup, the principal prize at this meeting, has for some years ranked as second in importance only to the Grand National. It has provided some heart-stirring contests, as that instanced between Golden Miller and Thomond II, and if this year's finish between the two Irish nine-year-olds, Cottage Rake and Happy Home, which the former won by one and a half lengths had not quite the same epic quality it was a magnificent contest, and up to the traditions of the race, for it was all round one of the best class fields of recent years, and it was run at a great pace throughout. . . . First and second were ridden respectively by Aubrey Brabazon and Martin Molony, two of Ireland's leading horsemen. This is the sort of race that warms the heart – two very good horses ridden by two very good jockeys, all four at top of their form, engaged in a close finish before a wildly and rapturously excited crowd. It is events such as this that make steeplechasing the eternally fascinating sport it is.'

If the correspondent of the *Irish Horse* thought the race fell short of epic, he did not have to wait long before for one that did not, for the very next year we find him writing of the Cheltenham Gold Cup,

'The contest was epic, tremendous even if it lacked a little of the longdrawn tenseness of the now legendary duel between Golden Miller and Thomond II fourteen years before. Only one was within hail of Cottage Rake and Cool Customer as they came round the bottom turn, and he was down with three fences out. Cool Customer, who had taken the lead after the second fence, was a length or so in front, but Aubrey Brabazon always had Cottage Rake in a striking position. He struck at the last, over which his rival landed slightly in front. Brabazon sat down to ride one of those great finishes in which strength, skill and judgment all play their part. It was probably even more obvious to the jockey than it was to the spectators that Cool Customer was only to be beaten by a super effort on the part of Cottage Rake, for P. J. Murphy was riding on the former and the horse was putting in everything he knew. It was just the extra little bit of speed that Cottage Rake had that enabled him to best his most formidable rival, but he was only complete master of the situation fifty yards from the post.'

Cottage Rake came out again in 1950 to win the Cheltenham Gold Cup once more and to beat Finnure by ten lengths.

The Gold Cup provided another great race and a stirring finish the following year when Lord Bicester's Silver Flame by Werwolf registered another victory for the descendants of Marco. In a desperate finish Silver Flame beat Greenogue by a short head. Silver Flame was a good chaser over park courses and, although he on one occasion started favourite for the Grand National, he was never able to get round the Aintree course.

Werwolf, the sire of Bogskar and Silver Flame, was bred by Sir Robert Jardine and was out of a half sister of the great mare Cinna, winner of the One Thousand Guineas and dam of the famous stallions so successful when exported to New Zealand, Beau Pere and his brothers. Werwolf sired the brilliant and spectacular chaser Aigead Sios, Timber Wolf, winner of the Welsh Grand National, Free Fare, a top-class hurdler who won the Manchester November Handicap, and many other well-known chasers.

In 1951 and again in 1953 the winners of the Grand National were bred from mares of the same line of 'jumping blood'. The first was Nickel Coin out of Viscum, a chestnut mare by Walter

Gay, a grandson of Hurry On. Before the National, Nickel Coin had proved herself a good and safe jumper. The start was a bad one, many of the runners being caught flat-footed, so there was a desperate dash for the first fence to make up lost ground. Horses went down and others fell over them, but J. Bullock on Nickel Coin cleverly avoided disaster and, although he had to snatch the mare to the left, she galloped on safely. Gay Heather was first over the water as they came round the first time with Nickel Coin second and the white-faced Royal Tan third. Gay Heather fell at Becher's and the race developed into a duel between the other two. They came to the last fence together but Royal Tan blundered badly leaving the race to Nickel Coin.

Two years later Early Mist out of Sudden Dawn, a daughter of Hurry On, won. Sudden Dawn ran six times unplaced as a two-year-old and was sold for 27 guineas. Her stud career meant nothing until she was covered by Brumeux. She foaled Early Mist, who was bought by J. V. Rank. He won a few races but fell on his first attempt in the National. At the dispersal sale brought about by Rank's death, he was bought by J. Griffin. Early Mist won a three-mile chase at Naas early in March only to be disqualified, then Bryan Marshall went over to Ireland to ride the horse in his work. He was completely satisfied and it was with high hopes that Vincent O'Brien, who had won the Cheltenham Gold Cup with Knock Hard, sent Early Mist over. Passing the stands over the water, the top weight, Mont Tremblant in Dorothy Paget's colours, led from the favourite, Little Yid, and Early Mist. Little Yid fell at the fence before Valentine's and the race was between the other two. With four fences to go Early Mist was clear with Mont Tremblant tiring under his big weight. Early Mist made a slight mistake at the penultimate fence but recovered to clear the last fence and went on to win by twenty lengths from the gallant, tired top weight.

We have now moved some generations away from Marco and his National Winner, Sprig, so we must return to the flat to pick up the story of the Matchem line handed on by Marco's son, Marcovil.

CHAPTER 7

HURRY ON

Marcovil was a strongly made chestnut of quality with a blaze. Unfortunately he inherited his sire's defective forelegs and so had to be very lightly raced. He did not appear on the racecourse until he was four and only ran four times in all. He won three of his races and was second in the other. He was still unnamed and it was in the name of his dam, as the Lady Villikins' colt, that he won his first race at Newmarket by four lengths from Tebworth in May 1907. Then, in much better company, he ran second beaten half a length in the Kempton Park Jubilee. Next time out he appeared for the first time as Marcovil and, at odds of 7.2 on, won a handicap at Gatwick by two lengths from Succory, with Simonson five lengths away third. Finally, following in his father's footsteps he won the Cambridgeshire in 1908.

The second decade of this century produced three horses each with a claim to being 'the best ever'. The flying The Tetrarch, Hurry On and Gay Crusader, winner of the 'Triple Crown'; all were unbeaten. It is possible that The Tetrarch might not have stayed – the Guineas winners that he sired, Tetratema and Mr Jinks, and the 'Flying Filly' Mumtaz Mahal suggest that – but he also sired Caligula, Polemarch and Salmon Trout, all three of whom had the stamina to win the St Leger over a mile and threequarters. It is true that Magpie got close to Gay Crusader in the Guineas but Gay Crusader's subsequent improvement was phenomenal. Nothing ever got close enough to Hurry On to give any idea of his capabilities and there was no doubt of his stamina. Marcovil's massive son was out of the minute Toute Suite, who was less than 15 hh and was considered too small to go into training, yet her son, Hurry On, stood 16.3 hh as a three-year-old and over 17 hh when he fully matured. He was a magnificent specimen, a throwback to Barcaldine, both physically and, unfortunately, temperamently. After being bought for 500 guineas by James Buchanan (later Lord Woolavington), he was trained by Fred Darling at Beckhampton. He never ran as a two-year-old in 1915. So difficult was he to manage that he had never been galloped upsides with another horse before his first race and had only been through the starting barrier once. In this race, over a mile at Lingfield, he dwelt at the start through inexperience but strolled past the other runners as he liked. He followed this victory with others over a mile and a half at Newmarket and a mile and quarter at Newbury, which race he won by three lengths with the One Thousand Guineas winner, Lord Derby's Canyon, third another five lengths behind. He was then tried for the St Leger over the Leger distance. The other horses in the trial were given six or seven lengths start, but Hurry On caught them with ease and won going away. The second in the trial had only shortly before been beaten by only a neck in the Newbury Cup and was getting 3 stone and a year from Hurry On, who was shouldering 9 stone 12 lbs! He won the St Leger, run as the September Stakes at Newmarket due to the war, in a canter from Clarissimus, who had won the Two Thousand Guineas. He then won the Newmarket St Leger and the Jockey Club Cup. Unfortunately, his high spirits or his bad temper, call it what you will, would not allow him to accept discipline. This temperament combined with his huge frame rendered him impossible to manage; his trainer was his only master, so he was retired to stud. Fred Darling said of him, 'the best horse I have ever seen, the best I am ever likely to see'. How good he was no one can tell, for there was no horse of his time capable of extending him. After having ridden a few winners as an apprentice, peppery little Fred Darling began training in 1907, then went to Germany, returning to take over the Beckhampton stable on the retirement of his father in 1913. A man so dedicated to his proffession that he had no personal friends, he was a complete autocrat, and even discouraged his owners from coming to the stable to see their horses

Hurry On may have dwelt in his first race but he was most certainly quick off the mark at stud, for he sired a Derby winner from the first mare he covered. The colt foal she dropped to the service of Hurry On took after his sire in size and substance. He was a massive chestnut with a blaze and three white stockings, but if Captain Cuttle took after his sire physically, he couldn't have been more different in temperament. The big fellow was as quiet as a kitten and would follow his trainer, Fred Darling, around hanging on to his coat sleeve with his teeth. Captain Cuttle only ran once as a two-year-old, finishing second to Collaborator at Doncaster in September. This was a good performance for a big, green colt, but after the race he developed a weakness in his knees, which, considering how heavy topped he was, is not surprising. Fred Darling wisely put him away till the following year, using him as a hack during the winter. In his classic year he came out in the Wood Ditton Stakes, so often the debut for maidens, which he won easily by six lengths. Shortly before the Two Thousand Guineas he suffered from a digestive complaint and was not at his best. Nevertheless, he ran well, finishing third to St Louis and Pondoland.

At Epsom he looked magnificent and in appearance completely outclassed the two that had finished in front of him in the Guineas, in looks he already had his race won. Leaving the paddock 'The Captain' began to walk lame. Steve Donoghue jumped from his back and found that one of his plates had spread. Whilst the other runners made their way to the start, the big chestnut remained behind in the paddock with the farrier hastily fitting a new shoe. He came out and cantered past the stands; he was still lame and the memory of his knee trouble the previous season cast a foreboding that all was not well. Richard Marsh writes,

> 'Perhaps the most marvellous thing that I ever saw was the Derby being won very easily by what at first glance I thought was the lamest horse that I ever saw go to the post. I am thinking of Captain Cuttle in 1922 . . . I saw him lame going to the post I would not have taken a thousand to one about his chance.'

As Donoghue went to the post he kept Captain Cuttle moving,

giving him a short sharp burst on the way. The lameness gradually wore off and his jockey put it down to stiffness due to standing on one foreleg while the farrier was shoeing the other. The field which awaited Captain Cuttle at the post was a good one but in the race none of them had a chance with him. 'Once round Tattenham Corner,' writes Steve Donoghue, 'I went straight out in front, as having still a lurking fear of a possible breakdown in my horse, I thought I would go out as far as I could, so that, in the event of any mishap, I might be far enough ahead to win in spite of it.' Luckily no such disaster occurred and Captain Cuttle passed the post four lengths in front of Tamar (Lord Astor, as usual, being the owner of the second). 'The Captain' was one of the easiest winners of the Derby and he set up a new record time for the race. 'I had a very easy ride,' writes Steve, 'but I must say I was sore all over afterwards with the strain I had put on my muscles in holding such a big, massive horse together to keep him balanced round those turns.'

And so Captain Cuttle was the first of the three white-faced chestnut sons of Hurry On that were to win the Derby. He went on to win the St James's Palace Stakes at Ascot but after that tendon trouble kept him at home for the rest of the season, so he missed the St Leger. The following year he appeared only once, to win the Prince of Wales Stakes at Kempton Park, but his forelegs were not up to carrying his massive frame and he could not contest the Ascot Gold Cup so he retired to stud. We really are writing of another time and another world when it was seriously thought that a Derby winner must, by custom, run in the Leger and the Gold Cup!

Captain Cuttle started well enough in his new role getting the One Thousand Guineas winner, Scuttle, in his first crop and the Derby second, Walter Gay, in the next and also, Glenabatrick, dam of a winner of the Ascot Gold Cup, in Tiberius. After these two seasons he was sold to Italy, where he died five years later in an accident while covering a mare. Roger Mortimer writes of him, 'He was a grand stamp of horse, well above the average standard of Derby winners and he might well have made a great name for himself at stud had he remained in this country.' Scuttle was bred by King George V out of Stained Glass, a daughter of Tracery, and was His Majesty's only classic winner. Great hopes had been entertained about Stained Glass, but she fell at exercise and damaged her pelvis. The unfortunate filly spent a long time in slings but her life was saved and she bred four winners. Scuttle won three of her five races as a two-year-old and was, perhaps, a little unlucky to be beaten in the Queen Mary Stakes at Ascot. During the winter Scuttle improved a lot and started favourite for the One Thousand Guineas. She was troublesome at the start and, eventually when the gate went up, lost three or four lengths. Joe Childs was in no hurry to make up the lost ground and, at half way, was still sitting still on her. From this point she improved rapidly and at the Bushes was second behind Jurisdiction; a good race home followed and Scuttle, running on with great gameness, worried Lord Dewar's filly out of it to win by a length. Toboggan was no less than seven lengths behind in third place. Lord Derby's Toboggan was a daughter of Hurry On. Although she had won the Dewhurst Stakes the previous season, she was still a very backward filly and it was considered that she had too much improvement to make up to have any chance of beating Scuttle in the Oaks. Hopes were high therefore for a Royal victory at Epsom and Scuttle started a hot favourite at even money. Scuttle, on this occasion, behaved well at the gate and coming to Tattenham Corner she was going easily in second place, but two and a half furlongs out it was obvious that Toboggan was going the better of the two and the latter raced away to win easily by four lengths. R. C. Lyle in *Royal Newmarket* writes,

'The crowd was almost frozen in silence. For the time being they could not realise that such a greatly anticipated winner had been beaten, and so well beaten. No one was more surprised than Lord Derby, who hardly dared to hope that his filly could have made so much improvement in six weeks as to reverse the previous running so completely.'

Toboggan proved her superiority again, and just as easily, when she beat Scuttle in the Coronation Stakes at Ascot. After two more defeats Scuttle retired to stud, where she died after having only four foals, of whom only two were winners, the best being Fairlead, a useful staying handicapper.

Captain Cuttle's daughter, Glenabatrick, foaled Tiberius to that great sire of stayers, Foxlaw. Tiberius was a very useful three-year-old, winning four races and finishing fourth in the Derby and second in the St Leger to Windsor Lad. The task of keeping the Ascot Gold Cup in England the next season against the formidable challenge of the great French champion Brantome fell to Sir Abe Bailey's colt. The Frenchman was an awe-inspiring opponent indeed. Unbeaten as a two-year-old, the next season he won the French Two Thousand Guineas, the Prix Lupin, the Royal Oak, in spite of being badly bumped, and the Prix de l'Arc de Triomphe from a star-studded field that included Asterus, Admiral Drake and Felicitation. He had won twelve races off the reel when he was sent over to compete for the Ascot Gold Cup. On paper, therefore, Tiberius's task looked very stiff but there was one thing in his favour and that was the going, which was hock deep. Brantome was by Blandford, and to me at least, it seemed unlikely that a son of Blandford would see out two and a half miles in going so deep. It was Tiberius, revelling in the mud and running like a true son of Foxlaw, who saw out every inch of the distance and came storming home alone. It was said of Brantome that he was not at his best as he had had an anti-tetanus injection after escaping in the Chantilly Forest; this might have been so, but in my opinion the way in which Tiberius carried home the black and gold hoops appeared invincible and I doubt if there was any horse that could have beaten Tiberius over that distance in the conditions that afternoon. Tiberius won the Goodwood Cup as well and then retired to stud, where he was not successful, although showing some prominence as a broodmare sire.

Hurry On's second Derby winner was again a big chestnut horse with a white face. Coronach was out of Wet Kiss by Tredennis, a very successful cross for Hurry On's third Derby winner, Call Boy, was out of a mare by Bachelor's Double by Tredennis and the Ascot Gold Cup winner Precipitation was out of another daughter of Bachelor's Double. Coronach was a lovely-looking horse but had a slightly ewe neck. Like his father, he had a mind of his own and was a desperately hard puller. He was trained by Fred Darling for his owner-breeder, Lord Woolavington. He won his first three races before being beaten in the Middle Park Stakes by Lex. He progressed well during the winter and won his first race the next season and so was made a hot favourite for the Two Thousand Guineas, in which race he was destined to meet Colorado, the horse that became his great rival. Lord Derby's Colorado was a very neat brown colt out of a half-sister of Toboggan's dam. He had opened the season by winning the Union Jack Stakes at his owner's home meeting but after that had put up a bad gallop the week before the Guineas and so had gone out in the market. Coronach gave some trouble at the start and was not too well away in the Guineas but he immediately pulled himself to the front and was in a clear lead at the Bushes. Coming into the Dip he was tackled by Colorado. Coronach found nothing extra so Colorado went on to win decisively. Lord Derby's colt was made favourite for the Derby.

Derby day was wet and dismal, something the public was growing used to, and the going was heavy. Coronach went down to the post in most taking style in conditions that obviously suited him. He jumped straight out in front and went clear of the field. He raced away to the top of the hill and led down to Tattenham Corner, where a dog ran yapping across the track. Joe Childs on Coronach managed to avoid it and slipped his field. Tommy Weston on Colorado was not so lucky and by the time he had got past the dog, he had no hope of catching Coronach. He frankly admits that he gave up the chase and, dropping his hands, was caught napping by Lancegaye for second place.

Coronach went on to win the St James's Palace Stakes at Ascot and the Eclipse just as easily, and so naturally became a hot favourite at odds-on for the St Leger. Joe Childs adopted the same tactics as he had at Epsom, sending Coronach out in front, but the big colt tore away to such purpose that his jockey was seriously worried that he would run himself out. In the straight a policeman stepped out from the rails and Coronach, sighting him, checked slightly, enabling Childs to get a hold on him and give him a breather. The big colt stormed up the straight to win impressively. I saw the race from down the course; admittance was free on the Town Moor, as it was to the Knavesmire, an important matter to me in those days! Right opposite me, broken down and standing on three legs, was Sir Abe Bailey's grand-looking colt Lex, a sad sight.

Coronach then retired for the season and came out next for the Coronation Cup, for which he started at 100–30 on. Those who laid the odds must have had some anxious moments as he only just managed to beat Embargo. In fact, Sidney Galtrey thinks that if Steve Donoghue on Embargo had not adopted waiting tactics but had forced the pace or disputed the lead with Coronach, he might well have beaten the favourite. In view of Coronach's form in his last two races this supposition might well be correct. After winning the Hardwicke Stakes at Ascot by twelve lengths, Coronach went to Newmarket in the hope of collecting the Prince of Wales Stakes without effort. Two days before the race, the event was one of little significance, but the day before it suddenly aroused great interest. There was a change of plans at Stanley House; it was announced that Colorado would run. Colorado had just won the Newbury Summer Cup easily by four lengths showing that he was back to his best. If he could not beat Coronach, it was thought that he would at least extend him.

Coronach took the lead as usual but this time Colorado was kept in touch and was never more than two lengths back. After nine furlongs Childs took an uneasy look over his shoulder to find Colorado closer than he would have liked. A moment later a shout went up from the stands, Colorado was upsides and, in a few strides, had his head in front. Childs asked Coronach to reply to the challenge but Colorado strode remorselessly ahead to win by eight lengths. What had happened to Coronach, hailed as one of the best of all time, to finish second best, and a bad second best, to Colorado? Admittedly Colorado had beaten him in the Guineas and it is true that Colorado had not liked the soft going when he, in his turn, was beaten at Epson. But was Colorado so much better? George Lambton was of the opinion that with the severity of the pace the horses were tired, and the one that cracked first would be easily beaten. Fred Archer had told him of a similar race between Ormonde and Minting in the Two Thousand Guineas: 'When you get two smashing good horses trying to cut one another down the pressure is so great that one or the other is sure to crack a long way from home; it may be a toss up which gives way first, but the one who does has no struggle left.'

Now came what was expected to be one of the greatest of matches of all time, the meeting of the two rivals in the Eclipse. A large crowd turned up at Sandown; the betting revealed little: 11–10 Coronach, 10–11 Colorado, with the other runner, Mario, at 25–1. Coronach got up to his old tricks at the start and it was quite a time before Childs could coax him up to the barrier and then he was slowly away. He was up in the lead quickly, two lengths clear of Colorado. So they ran, until a quarter of a mile from home. Weston, on Colorado, made his effort; in a few strides he was level with the leader. There was a tussle before Coronach cracked and Colorado went on to win by six lengths. Poor Coronach was not even second; so tired was he that he was passed by the only other runner, the moderate maiden Mario. So Coronach was completely dethroned. It may be that he did not like to struggle, it may that he had gone in the wind or, it may be that he had met his match in Colorado, that the latter was the better horse and that, as Archer and Lambton said, when one of two smashing good colts cracks the other wins easily.

At stud, Coronach did not do much in his own country, but he has a fine record internationally. In France, Italy and Germany his sons and daughters won big races. Due to the war he was not fully patronised in England and so was sent to New Zealand, where his progeny – Coronaise, Balgowan, Western Front and My Bonnie – won four classics. The greatest of his produce was the filly Corrida, bred by Marcel Boussac. It was ironical that such a great internationalist as Corrida should herself fall victim to warring nations. She was a much-travelled filly, successful in France, England, Belgium and Germany. Corrida took after her sire in colouring: she was a chestnut with a blaze, stockings on her off fore and near hind and a white fetlock on her off hind. In France Corrida was reckoned the best two-year-old filly of 1934, a pound ahead of Mesa, who came to England to win the One Thousand Guineas. Corrida was sent to be trained in England, where she was most disappointing, finishing last in the One Thousand Guineas and being unplaced in the Oaks and at Ascot. She returned to France and showed much improved form winning the

Grand Prix de Marseilles and being placed in three of France's top races. As a four-year-old Corrida showed her brilliance by winning races: five races in France, including the Prix de l'Arc de Triomphe, the Hardwicke Stakes in England, the Brown Ribbon in Germany and Grand International d'Ostende in Belgium. Corrida raced again for a fourth season, with a magnificent finish to her career by winning the Prix de L'Arc de Triomphe for the second time. When she retired to stud she had won more stakes in France than any other horse had earned up to that time, let alone her winnings in other countries.

Corrida was a lovely mare, full of quality and even-tempered. Her only fault was a tendency to in and out running, brilliant victories often being followed by disappointments. She only had one foal before falling into German hands. That one showed what a broodmare she might have become for it was the French Derby winner, Coaraze. Baron de Gelsey describes him as a 'small horse with a lion's heart'. He had somewhat the same failing as his dam, in that he did not always maintain his best form but, besides the French Derby, he won the Grand Prix de Saint Cloud, the Grand Prix de Vichy and eight other races. Another brilliant daughter of Coronach was Jacopo del Sellaio, who won all the Italian classics except their St Leger.

Another of the progeny of Coronach who was a war victim was the bay Cranach, who was bred by Baron Guy de Rothschild and stolen by the Germans. He won eleven races in Germany but went to stud in France after he had been liberated. He got many top-class horses including Flute Enchantee, who won the Grand Prix de Deauville by six lengths, Violoncello, Craneur, Ombrette, Ciel Etoile and Pas de Calais.

One of Coronach's best two sons was Niccolo dell'Arca, a half-brother of Nearco, and bred by Tesio. Niccolo dell'Arca raced during the war and won three of his six races at two years old, including the Gran Criterium by eight lengths. At three he was invincible, winning all his seven races without being extended, including the Italian two Thousand Guineas and the Italian Derby by twenty lengths in record time. He also won the Grosser Preis der Reichshaupstadt in Germany. Of the two great sons of Nogara, Tesio considered Nearco to be the more brilliant and Niccolo dell'Arca to be the better stayer. At stud he got two top-class fillies who were contemporaries, Astolfina and Trevisana, the latter being a half-sister of Ribot. Trevisana won seven races as a three-year-old, including the Italian St Leger and the Gran Premio d'Italia. Astolfina, the same season, won the Italian One Thousand, the Italian Oaks and the Gran Premio de Milano, in which race she beat both Trevisana and Tenerani, who later was to win the Goodwood Cup and sire Ribot. Niccolo dell'Arca's best son was Daumier, who was unbeaten in Italy and went to stud in the United States.

In England, the best of Coronach's sons were not of classic calibre. They were Montrose and the gelding Highlander, who won twenty-one races. Montrose, a chestnut colt, was a useful but not brilliant racehorse, winning such races as the City and Suburban. He was dead game and Sir Gordon Richards describes him as 'that grand little horse, Montrose'. As might have been expected of a horse of this class, he was not patronised by the best in his own country, but it was found that his stock had only to put their feet on the ground in South Africa to start winning races. The record of the imported stock of Montrose is incredible. From 39 runners he had 32 winners of 171 races. When it is remembered that these horses were only eligible to race in top- or near top-class handicaps this record is remarkable. Between 1947 and 1953 the Durban Gold Cup, the premier long-distance race in the country, went to sons of Montrose on five occasions, and the Durban July, at that time the most valuable race in the country, four times between 1944 and 1950. Moreover, Montrose headed the sires list in a country other than that in which he was standing, a remarkable feat before the regular transport of racehorses by air. The phenomenal success of Montrose's imported progeny prompted the importation of Montrose himself but the experiment was not successful.

After Coronach's Derby victory, it was not long before another son of Hurry On and another white-faced chestnut had won the Derby, for the very next year the well-named Call Boy out of Comedienne was victorious. Call Boy was engaged in a desperately close finish for the Two Thousand Guineas, in which he had probably worn himself out in a long battle with Hot Night. Jack

Leach on Adam's Apple watching the two leaders from wide out across the course had put in a beautifully timed challenge to win by a short head on Adam's Apple. Call Boy had been hand ridden, Charlie Elliot not wanting to give the colt a hard race on his first outing of the season. Had Charlie Elliott hit him, he might have pulled out enough to win; on the other hand he might have resented it.

Between the Guineas and the Derby, Call Boy won the Newmarket Stakes and at Epsom started favourite at slightly shorter odds than Hot Night, who meanwhile had won at York. The customary Derby dinner was held at the Press with Edgar Wallace in the chair. Responding to the toast of 'The Derby Stakes', Frank Curzon, the owner of Call Boy, said that he sincerely believed that his horse was 5–7 lbs better than any three-year-old in England. Sir Victor Sassoon, the owner of Hot Night, was the next to respond and said, 'I have a hope that on Wednesday he will have the right to carry his head as high as some of you maintain he does in his races.' Lord Derby, the owner of Sickle, then said,

> 'The horse is very fit and well. So is every other horse in the race. The owner is satisfied and thoroughly confident. Ditto every other owner. The trainer is completely satisfied. Ditto every other trainer. The jockeys are all pleased with their respective mounts. Nothing could be better. I hope the best horse will win and I hope it will prove to be mine.'

Lord Birkenhead, replying to the toast to 'The Guests', said, 'We have heard a lot of nonsense about everybody wanting the best horse to win. They do not want the best horse to win. They want their own horse to win.'

It was a fine day at Epsom for a change and the going was perfect, as Lord Derby had said, nothing could be better. Elliott sent Call Boy straight away into the lead. Once in the straight Hot Night improved and, for a few moments, actually headed Call Boy, but the latter responded to Elliott's urgings and drew out to win by two lengths. Despite being desperately ill, Call Boy's owner, Frank Curzon, gallantly would not forgo the pleasure of leading in his Derby winner, but within a short time he was dead and, under the absurd old rule, Call Boy's nomination for the St Leger became void.

These were the days of Tom Webster's wonderful cartoons in the *Daily Mail* and he recorded the celebration dinner given by the winning jockey to the fellow members of his profession:

'Practically every jockey in the world made a speech. Fred Fox, who was in the chair, said he was glad Charlie Elliott had won the Derby. Then Brownie Carslake said that, as he hadn't won it himself, he was glad Charlie Elliott had won the Derby. Shaking a wicked knife and fork, Steve Donoghue said he was glad Charlie Elliott had won the Derby. Shaking himself almost to pieces Gordon Richards said he was glad Charlie Elliott had won the Derby. Then Johnny Dines said he was glad Charlie Elliott had won the Derby. Victor Smyth said he too was glad Charlie Elliott had won the Derby. Sheff Wragg (the rider of the second) said he was perfectly satisfied that Charlie Elliott had won the Derby. Jack Leach said he was more than glad that Charlie Elliott had won the Derby. In a speech full of brilliant phrases George Duller said he was glad that Charlie Elliott had won the Derby. Then Charlie Elliott said he was glad that he had won the Derby. Being seen home at a very late hour Call Boy said that, although it came as a bit of shock to find that he hadn't won the Derby, he congratulated Charlie Elliott nevertheless.'

The sale of Call Boy after Frank Curzon's death was a matter of great interest to many, and it was with relief that it was learnt that Call Boy would remain to go to stud in England. Satisfaction at this turned to dismay when it was found that Call Boy was practically sterile. His daughter, aptly named Last Act, bred Ended to Felicitation, the horse who beat Hyperion in the Ascot Gold Cup. Ended won twenty-six races in California, breaking the track record for six furlongs at Hollywood Park, a surprising performance in view of the stout staying blood on both sides of the pedigree.

In 1919 the newly formed National Stud bred Diligence by Hurry On. Like others from the stud he was leased to Lord Lonsdale. He was a backward colt and did not make his first appearance until he was three, when he ran in the Newmarket Stakes. Diligence ran very green, swerving badly and finishing unplaced. Somewhat ambitiously, he was started for the Derby, starting at 50–1 and running well down the course. At even money he won the Sussex Stakes at Goodwood, a race which was not of the same importance as it is today. He started for the St Leger at a shorter price than Royal Lancer, another product of the National Stud, running in the colours of the Yellow Earl, as Lord Lonsdale was known from his coach, his fleet of yellow motor cars and his kennel of numerous golden labradors. Royal Lancer scored the first classic win for the National Stud, for the owner and for the jockey, Bobby Jones; his stable companion was well down the course. Diligence won the Newmarket St Leger. – unfortunately for me as I had a shilling on my uncle's horse, Silver Band, who ran second. The next season, Diligence only ran twice, dead-heating for the Kempton Park Jubilee with Simon Pure and winning the Newbury Summer Cup. He then retired to the National Stud. Many of his stock were ungenuine, blamed on the strain of Cheshire Cat, his grandam, and he was sold abroad but not before he had sired Clarence, which is really why Diligence is mentioned here. Clarence was out of a mare by Friar Marcus, who had done so well for King George V, so it was fitting that Clarence's daughter, Sun Chariot, should have been leased by his son, King George VI. It was a wonderful thing that during the gloom of the World War we should have been cheered by the victories of two such good horses as Big Game and Sun Chariot running in the royal colours but it was a pity that they were contemporaries. Big Game, winner of the Two Thousand Guineas, was a good horse with stamina limitations, whereas the daughter of Clarence, Sun Chariot, was a great filly - Sir Gordon Richards said the greatest he ever rode. Had Big Game not been in the stable that year, King George VI would have won the Derby as well as the Oaks with Sun Chariot. Brilliant as she was, she was a right bitch, and only brilliant when she felt like it. At Salisbury she just refused to gallop, staying tucked in behind the other horses, with her tail swishing round and round like a windmill. In the Oaks she could not have behaved worse, when the barrier eventually rose she remained at the post while the field streamed away. In Sir Gordon's words,

> 'The field must have gone a furlong before I had covered much more than fifty yards. Then she caught sight of the other horses, and decided to straighten out and follow them. I thought it was quite hopeless. You can imagine my feelings of disappointment, particularly as Their Majesties were watching. I remember thinking how very disappointed the king must be, looking through his glasses from the other end of the course. After we had gone nearly a mile Sun Chariot reached the end of the field. Then she began to thread her way through them. I suddenly began to have hope again. Three furlongs from home she was up with the leaders. She was going so well that I decided to let her canter on – no more Salisbury disasters through interfering with this wayward miss! She went straight on and won nicely by a length. It was one of the most amazing performances I have ever known.'

In the St Leger she proved what a certainty she would have been for the Derby had she been started, for she beat the Derby winner, Watling Street, with the greatest of ease by three lengths.

Diligence had a full brother called Feridoon, also bred at the National Stud. There was a deal of criticism when he was sold privately to the Aga Khan instead of being offered by public auction, although the price paid was a record one for a yearling. The National Stud got the best of the bargain, as Feridoon was a useless racehorse and was said to have been sold for a thousandth of his cost as a yearling to a Paris cab driver, who took clients for rides behind what he called 'the million franc horse'. One would have thought that would have been the last heard of Feridoon but, just as his brother did, one of his daughters bred a good horse and he appears as the maternal grandsire of the good stayer Deux Pour Cent, who raced in France during the war. He won a couple of races before running fifth to Ardan in the French Derby. Ardan started at the exceedingly short price of 3–10 for the Grand Prix de Paris and passed the post a neck from Deux Pour Cent, but the siren was quickly sounded and Deux Pour Cent got the race.

Ardan won the Prix de l'Arc de Triomphe with Deux Pour Cent third. At stud Deux Pour Cent achieved fame as the sire of a really good horse in Tantieme.

Hurry On's daughters brought him as much fame as his Derby-winning sons, for besides Toboggan, who scuttled the King's filly in the Oaks, he sired three other classic-winning fillies. Lord Rosebery's Plack was a typical offspring of her sire, chestnut in colour and a grand stayer, a game hard-working mare. She ran twenty-six times, winning nine races and being placed eleven times. Roger Mortimer, the well-known racing correspondent, writes of her,

> 'Plack invariably swished her tail round and round like a propeller in the closing stages of a race. In her case it was certainly no sign of unwillingness, as there can be few mares tougher or gamer than she was. Like most great racemares she had her idiosyncrasies and never in her life would she be ridden under Newmarket railway bridge. Invariably they had to dismount and lead her.'

The One Thousand Guineas which she won was the one in which Mumtaz Mahal, 'The Flying Filly', started a short-priced favourite. 'Mumty' was lengths in front at the Bushes but a half furlong later Plack and Straitlace had begun to reduce her lead. At the foot of the rise to the winning post, the favourite had had more than enough, she changed her legs and became unbalanced. Plack raced up to her and past her to win by a length and a half. In the Oaks Plack ran second to Straitlace, who had been third in the One Thousand. There was a strong French challenge for the Ascot Gold Cup in which Massine and Filibert de Savoie ran first and second. According to Charlie Smirke, her jockey, Plack might well have held the challenge at bay. Papyrus tried to force his way through between the filly and the rails. The bump she then received threw Plack out of her stride and upset her so much that it was some time before she could get going again. Smirke maintained that but for this mishap Plack would have won the race. At stud, Plack produced Coin of the Realm, dam of the Derby second Midas. After producing another winner Plack was barren for many years until at last she produced a foal appropriately named Afterthought, who followed in her mother's foot-steps by running second in the Oaks and winning the Jockey Club Cup. Plack was trained by Jack Jarvis, and bred by her owner, the 5th Earl of Rosebery at the Mentmore Stud in Hertfordshire. Lord Rosebery, who was Prime Minister in 1894–5, had won the Derby with Ladas (1894), Sir Visto (1895) and Cicero (1905), and married the daughter of Baron Meyer de Rothschild, founder of the Mentmore Stud.

The next of Hurry On's daughters to win a classic was Colonel Loder's Cresta Run. She was a brilliant filly on her day but all too often failed to produce her form. On her second appearance she started favourite for the National Produce Stakes on the strength of her home gallops but was unplaced. She showed her true worth when she won a high-class nursery and scored an outstanding win in the Imperial Produce Stakes by three lengths. She then ran stone last of twelve runners in the Middle Park in which she started a better favourite than Call Boy, who won. She was still rated the best filly in the Free Handicap and justified this by a brilliant win in the One Thousand Guineas. Cresta Run, a big muscular filly made all the running and with her smooth, graceful action toyed with the others, coming in two lengths, which she could have easily made more, clear of the dead-heaters Book Law and Endowment. In the Oaks the tapes were broken several times, which upset Cresta Run who was slowly away and came in last. Her trainer, P. P. Gilpin, wrote,

'She was a highly strung filly, irritable and capricious and nearly always on her toes ... On Oaks day she behaved in an exemplary manner until she broke out in a sweat just before leaving the paddock. The parade and the delay at the post did not mend matters. She, however, was well away in the false starts and looked like doing all right, but after the second breakaway would have none of it and was ignomini-ously left. There is no doubt in my mind that she was a brilliant filly, and that she would have beaten the colts as easily as she did the fillies had she met them and (most important of all) been in the humour to do so.'

Cresta Run ran in only one more race, starting favourite for the

Irish Oaks. She could not have run worse, showing a strong disinclination to start at all, and then refusing to put her heart into it.

Two years later a daughter of Hurry On won the Oaks. This was Pennycomequick, one of the legion of good racemares that used to come from Cliveden Stud almost as off an assembly line. Lord Astor's filly won her only race as a juvenile by five lengths at Newmarket. She missed the first fillies' classic and her first outing at three was in the Haverhill Stakes at Newmarket, in which she was both favourite and successful. Then followed her triumph in the Oaks, for which race she started favourite and beat the opposition pointless, winning with the greatest of ease by five lengths. The winner of the Oaks was made favourite for the St Leger as the colts of that year were not highly esteemed. I doubt if I have ever seen going as hard as it was on the Town Moor in 1929. The only horse who seemed really at home on the going was the Derby winner, Trigo, and he duly won his second classic from Bosworth and Horus, who was completely incapable of striding out. Pennycomequick ran fifth in this, her last race. At stud, she bred numerous winners, the best of whom were Pound Foolish and High Stakes. The former won the Princess of Wales's Stakes at Newmarket and ran fourth in the Derby. The other's name joined those of the many game geldings. He was so precocious that he was added to the list at two years old. He ran for nine seasons winning thirty-four races carrying weights up to 10 stone 3 lbs and being placed sixteen times. One of Pennycomequick's progeny that did not win was Penicuik, who went to America to Calumet Farm in foal to Hyperion. The foal, Pensive, won the Kentucky Derby in 1944. Retiring to stud at Calumet, Pensive sired Ponder, who won the same American classic five years later.

We have seen how Toboggan beat Scuttle in the Oaks and again in the Coronation Stakes at Ascot. She had thus proved herself the best classic filly of the season and she was allowed to walk over the Welsh Oaks and then was strangely defeated in the St George Stakes. During a spell of dry weather the part of the course near the rails had been artificially watered, then came the rain. A lot of jostling took place during the race with all the jockeys trying to get off the false going on the soft ground. During the scrimmage Toboggan was pulled first this way and then the other, which she resented and thereafter refused to take any interest in the race. Her next and last race was the Jockey Club Stakes when she crowned her career and raised the question as to whether she might not be, not only the best filly, but also the best of her age; this is saying something as it was Fairway, who won the St Leger, who was the best of the colts. George Lambton, who managed both Fairway and Toboggan while Frank Butters trained them, pointed out that Toboggan had beaten Foliation as far as Coronach had beaten her. He writes that,

'There is no doubt that Coronach, Colorado, Fairway and Toboggan are of superior class to the three-year-olds of 1927, Call Boy, Hot Night, Beam and Book Law; also that Fairway is a better horse than Coronach or Colorado, and Toboggan is a better class mare than either Short Story or Beam, the Oaks winners of 1926 and 1927.'

This rates her very high indeed but he does not compare his colt with his filly. Nobody was better qualified to make such a judgment than Lambton, who had had almost a lifetime's experience of the Thoroughbred by 1928. Born in 1860, the fifth son of the 2nd Earl of Durham, he was a successful amateur steeplechase jockey before becoming the first man from his background to turn to training when taking charge of the stable of the 16th Earl of Derby in 1893. For the 17th Earl he won the Derby with Sansovino in 1924. Two years later he retired to manage the stable, but resumed training in 1930.

A mare, Hastily by Hurry On, was sold at the Newmarket Autumn Sales in foal to Lancegaye and went to the United States. The foal she was carrying, Cavalcade, as he was named, was the champion three-year-old of 1934. He won the Kentucky Derby from that good horse Discovery. In fact, he beat Discovery six times. Cavalcade also won the American Derby, the Detroit Derby and the Classic Stakes before developing a quarter crack in his hoof, which put him out of work and he never recovered his true form.

Hurry On's daughter Jiffy, whose owner the 6th Earl of Rosebery had inherited the title on the death of his father in 1929, was placed five times. After a few rather disappointing years at Mentmore, she produced Ocean Swell to Lord Rosebery's 1939 Derby winner Blue Peter in that famous horse's first year at stud. Ocean Swell ran disappointingly in the Guineas and so Lord Rosebery was merely hopeful about his chance in the Derby. He said, 'Had he not run in the Guineas I might have thought differently, because I knew he would stay every yard of the mile and a half.' There were much higher hopes for Growing Confidence, who was also by Blue Peter out of a daughter of Hurry On and who started favourite. Lord Rosebery, maybe influenced by the fact that the favourite was also by his stallion Blue Peter, released Eph Smith, the stable jockey, so that he could ride him and engaged Willy Nevett for Ocean Swell. Nevett had already ridden him in the Guineas, in which race Eph Smith had been on Honeyway, the more fancied of Jack Jarvis's two runners. The Yorkshire jockey came south again the next year to win the Derby on his own stable's Dante. Eph Smith, however, did not get the mount on the favourite but rode the Aga Khan's Tehran, who was later to win the St Leger. It was a dull, grey Derby Day on Newmarket Heath and the going was hard for what, to judge by the betting, looked to be a very open race and that is what it looked like being at half way. Tehran and Ocean Swell had joined His Excellency up in front; Growing Confidence and Garden Path were well placed, as were Happy Landing and Abbots Fell. Wood Cot was going well. Nevett, riding Ocean Swell, said,

'I moved up just before we raced down the hill, and I wanted to take the lead at that point, but my horse was not able to match the speed of Tehran. As soon as we began to climb the hill my mount ran on and, once he had taken the lead, I always felt like winning. He is a grand stayer.'

It was a great race home. Ocean Swell beating Tehran by a neck, with Happy Landing only a short head away third. Tehran got his revenge in the St Leger. The next season Ocean Swell won the Ascot Gold Cup, at last run at Ascot again, from Tehran who was a short-priced favourite. Sir Gordon Richards writes,

'Tehran was going beautifully. In fact he was going so well

that I let him go on into the lead coming into the straight. Then I sat there, waiting for Ocean Swell to challenge. But Mr Jack Jarvis had made his plans too well. As he entered the straight, Eph Smith took Ocean Swell right across the course to the Stands side, far away from me. I saw him too late. Tehran thought he had nothing to pull out the usual extra against. I tried to get over to Ocean Swell, but Eph had now got the first run on me and I could not get near him. So Ocean Swell won. That was a wonderful bit of planning, and it beat me and Tehran.'

Ocean Swell was the first Derby winner to win the Gold Cup at Ascot since Persimmon half a century before, and, alas, will be the last one.

Ocean Swell went to the Mentmore Stud, where he died as a young horse at thirteen. He was not a success, his best being Fastnet Rock, a good filly Sea Parrot and St Vincent, who was useful in the United States.

CHAPTER 8

'HE WUZ DE MOSTEST HORSE'

The best of all the good sons of Man o'War was the dark brown colt War Admiral. Like Crusader, he was bred at Faraway Farm by Samuel D. Riddle, who had bought Man o'War as a yearling. He won twenty of his twenty-six races. As a three-year-old in 1937 he had an unbeaten record, winning the Triple Crown of the Kentucky Derby, the Preakness and the Belmont, in which race, in spite of being injured, he equalled the American record set up by his sire. His successful career continued the next season and he was only beaten twice. One of these occasions was in his famous match with Seabiscuit.

For the moment we skip a generation to Seabiscuit as he was a bay colt by Man o'War's son Hard Tack. Seabiscuit was a year older than War Admiral and these two completely dwarfed their rivals in their respective classes and will go down among the truly greats bred in America. Seabiscuit did not mature early and his first outings showed no indication of the successes to come. After running fourth in his first race Seabiscuit was beaten by a maiden pony in a claiming race and it was not until his eighteenth outing that he could win a race and that was a claiming race. He then won three races in succession but he showed the same moderate form the next year when he won only two races in ten outings. After he had won a claiming race he was bought by Charles S. Howard for whom he won five races that season. Seabiscuit was beginning to come to hand. At four, in 1937, he won seven races off the reel, now in the big time and with big weights his form continued into his next year. War Admiral's activities during the winter were confined to Florida, while Seabiscuit went to the Pacific Coast to run in the Santa Anita Handicap, the richest race in the world. George 'the Iceman' Woolf, Seabiscuit's jockey, lost his cool on this occasion when Seabiscuit got slammed coming out of the gate and was knocked out of it. As the champion American jockey Johnny Longden said, 'George was mad and worried, and on the back stretch he was so far out of it he moved too soon – passed the entire field. But he'd taken too much out of "The Biscuit", and they lost to Stagehand by a nose.' Stagehand, who was unquestionably the best three-year-old of his year, was by Lord Derby's Sickle out of a daughter of Fair Play. Seabiscuit went on to win two big handicaps on the Pacific coast. The racing world was split as to which was the better, the son or the grandson of Man o'War. August Belmont scheduled a match, but Seabiscuit was withdrawn as his knees were troubling him. They were both entered for the Massachusetts Handicap, but Seabiscuit was withdrawn ten minutes before the race. Seabiscuit was then well beaten by War Minstrel in Chicago but went on westwards to win the Pacific Gold Cup. He was then matched with South American bred Ligarotti. There was a deal of sniffing and lifting of eyebrows at this as Ligarotti was owned by the son of the owner of Seabiscuit, in partnership with Bing Crosby. It was, however, a tremendous race, with Seabiscuit, after a terrific struggle, beating Ligarotti by a nose. After War Admiral had won the Jockey Club Cup at Belmont, the question of a match with Seabiscuit was again brought up, but the directors of Belmont, once bitten, would have nothing to do with it. Maryland Jockey Club then put on the match on 1st November 1938 at Pimlico, at level weights over eleven and a half furlongs and with a $10,000 forfeit to ensure they both turned up. War Admiral was long odds on, while Seabiscuit paid $6.20 to $2 on the tote. Seabiscuit looked very fit, but War Admiral a bit tucked up and his jockey, Kurtsinger, appeared nervous. At the third attempt a start was effected with War Admiral in the inside position jumping off on the wrong foot. Woolf immediately drew his whip and passing the stands the first time Seabiscuit was a length to the good. He got over to the rail and going into the back stretch was four lengths clear. Kurtsinger now drew his whip again and War Admiral began to close the gap, caught him on the last turn and poked his nose in front. Woolf once again went for his whip and a furlong and a half from home had managed to get half a length clear. The favourite was beaten and Seabiscuit began to draw away, so Kurtsinger dropped his hands and Seabiscuit went past the post four lengths clear to break the track record in 1 minute 56⅗. Neil Newman, in *Racing Since 1900*, records that War Admiral was 'badly managed, trained and ridden'. Seabiscuit was out of action for almost the whole of the next season but was brought out of more or less retirement to exceed the stakes earnings record of Sun Beau.

War Admiral was a great success at stud heading the sires list in 1945. Among his best known sons were War Jeep and Cable, but perhaps he is more famous for his daughters. Colonel Edward Riley Bradley of Idle Hour Farm, Lexington, Kentucky, whose fortune came from a Palm Beach casino, said he had a dislike for the Fair Play blood but, so impressed was he with War Admiral, that he sent two mares to him. He had every reason to be satisfied with his decision for the results were two rare good fillies, Busher and Bee Mac. Busher, a chestnut filly, was bred during the war years and she has been acclaimed as one of the greatest fillies to race in America during the present century. She was the unbeaten winner of five races as a juvenile and she then passed into the ownership of the film magnate Louis B. Mayer. She won ten races for him and, on terms worse than weight-for-age, she beat the good gelding Armed, in the Arlington Handicap. After winning three more top-class handicaps, she met with an accident and was unable to race again that season and was sold to Neil S. McCarthy. She ran once for her new owner but as she failed to show her form he sold her for $150,000, a record price for a filly, to Mrs 'Elizabeth Arden' Graham, who had given $50,000, a record price for a weanling, for her full brother, Mr Busher. Mr Busher became the equal best two-year-old of 1948, a title he shared with Blue Peter, another son of War Admiral. 'Elizabeth Arden' won the Kentucky Oaks with Fascinator, a granddaughter of War Admiral by War Jeep. Bee Mac, the other foal bred from the matings of Colonel Bradley's mares with War Admiral, won the Spinaway and $100,000. At stud she proved herself a great matron, foaling Better Self, winner of $382,925, Prophet's Thumb, winner of the

Discovery and the Pageant Handicaps, the brilliant sprinter Beau Max and other good horses.

The best known of War Admiral's daughters in England is Singing Grass as she was the dam of the Derby and St Leger winner, Never Say Die. Singing Grass was bred in America by R. Sterling Clark (the Singer sewing machine heir) but raced in England where she won three small races. She was out of a half-sister to Sterling Clark's One Thousand and Oaks winner, Galatea II. In 1951, Singing Grass bred her first foal, a chestnut with a blaze and three white feet who was named Never Say Die. Like his other horses Sterling Clark sent him to be trained in England. As a two-year-old he was useful but not brilliant, being allotted 8 stone 3 lbs in the Free Handicap. Although he started favourite, a moderate display in this race suggested that even this rating was too high. After this the colt began to improve rapidly and he was third in a close finish for the Newmarket Stakes. On form, his prospects for the Derby were not encouraging but he had a hidden asset, his rider was the eighteen-year-old Lester Piggott, whose first of many Derby winners this was. Coming round Tattenham Corner Lester had his mount handily placed behind the leaders. Once in the straight nothing had a chance with the American colt, who won by two lengths from John 'Airborne' Ferguson's Arabian Night and Darius. Although Never Say Die started at 33–1 Roger Mortimer tells us that it was a good race for the small punter as Lester already had a following and many others liked the winner's name.

Never Say Die's next race was a sensational one and is often recalled, as it resulted in the withdrawal of Lester Pigott's licence to ride. It was the King Edward VII Stakes at Ascot when Lester tried to force his way through, causing Arabian Night to stumble and hit the rails cannoning back on to the American-bred Blue Prince II, who in turn went on to Tarjoman, who bumped Rashleigh. Rashleigh, a grandson of Hurry On, went on to win from Blue Prince II and Tarjoman. It was on his next outing at Doncaster for the St Leger that the Derby winner showed that his Epsom win was no fluke. Joe Lawson had him looking a picture and Sterling Clark, who had made the journey from America to be present on the Town Moor, had every reason to feel proud of his colt. Ridden on this occasion by Charlie Smirke, he was waited with and in the straight simply shot away from his field; the official assessment of the distance by which he won, easing up, was twelve lengths. The almighty dollar has lured prospective stallions one after another from Britain, so it was with satisfaction and gratitude that British breeders learnt that Sterling Clark's Derby and St Leger winner would stand at the National Stud.

Man o'War, (by Fair Play, a son of the great broodmare Fairy Gold, out of a daughter of Rock sand) was mated to Friar's Carse, whose sire Friar Rock, was by Rock Sand out of Fairy Gold. This return of the blood of both Rock Sand and Fairy Gold, with only one free generation, resulted in three good performers – War Relic, War Kilt and Speed Boat. War Relic sired Battlefield, out of Dark Display, a daughter of Display. Battlefield won the Futurity, and was the best two-year-old of 1950, before going on to win the Withers, the Dwyer and big handicaps. The pedigree of Battlefield is of exceptional interest. The appearance of such a wonderful mare as Fairy Gold three times in the fourth remove must be very rare. In addition Battlefield is inbred to Fair Play with only two generations free.

The best daughter of Man o'War was Bateau, who ranks among the best American fillies of all time. Like War Relic she had a return of the blood of Fairy Gold. She won the Fashion and the Selima Stakes at two years old in 1927 and four races the next season including the Coaching Club Oaks, the American Oaks and the Gazelle Stakes. She won eleven races the next season and was second five times. Her stud career was a disaster: she could never be got into foal.

There are many other sons, daughters and grandchildren of Man o'War who deserve a mention but nothing like so many as there should be. His owner limited him to only twenty-five mares per season when he could have easily managed nearly three times as many; also he practically kept him for his own mares, which were a moderate lot. One of his sons that must be recalled is the gallant little chaser Battleship. Like many of the line he was a chestnut but, unlike so many of the line, he was a midget. Battleship was a top-class steeplechaser in the United States, where he stood at stud for a time before he crossed the Atlantic to win the

Grand National. The ability he had shown and the experience he had had over stiff timber fences in America stood him in good stead in England, and throughout the winter he jumped faultlessly, never taking a chance or making a mistake. By the time of the Grand National he had demonstrated that he must have an outstanding chance but the critics considered that his lack of inches would be a severe handicap over the Aintree fences and he was allowed to start at the generous odds of 40–1, at which price I helped myself. The race proved a victory for giant-killers, as the American stallion stood only 15.2 hh and his rider, Bruce Hobbs, was barely seventeen years old. The strong Irish horse, Royal Danieli, dominated the race for most of the way until another Irishman, Workman, began to catch him. The latter hit the last fence hard leaving Royal Danieli in a three-lengths lead and the race appeared to be over, but Bruce Hobbs brought Battleship with a strong run and the two horses crossed the line wide apart and impossible for the onlookers to separate them. When the numbers went up Battleship had won by a head.

When Man o'War retired to stud at Lexington, the great horse's box became the mecca of many pilgrimages and, even after his retirement from service in 1943, he still remained on view to the public. John Hervey ('Salvator') pays him this tribute,

'The death of Man o'War marks the end of an era in American turf and breeding history. For the past quarter of a century he may be said, in the words of the famous quotation, to have stridden our Thoroughbred world like a Colossus. His majestic form, towering high above all living horses, dominated the landscape, much as the gigantic statue of Apollo at ancient Rhodes, which among the seven wonders of the world as it then existed, was reckoned the most wonderful, so Man o'War among the Thoroughbreds of this century. The galaxy of stars that he sent out included horses of every age, sex and every species of performance. They have shown the most magnificent class over timber, while on the tan bark their individualities have brought them the blue upon numerous occasions in the most aristocratic competition. And here is the particular phase of Man o'War that stands out in bold relief: no other of the world's so-called super horses – neither Ormonde, nor St Simon, Gladiateur nor Carbine, Sardanaple, Phar Lap nor Gloaming in modern times, nor back all the way to Eclipse, Herod and Matchem – has possessed such a magnificent a front. No other has so completely looked the part or, simply in his own personality, enacted it so regally.'

Or, as his groom put it more simply, '*He wuz de mostest horse.*'

War Relic, who handed on the Matchem line, was foaled when Man o'War was twenty-one and was the last big race winner that 'Big Red' got. War Relic was by Man o'War out of Friar's Carse by Rock Sand out of Fairy Gold and so was inbred to both Rock Sand and Fairy Gold in the third remove and repeated the successful cross. Because of a strained back War Relic did not race until he was a three-year-old, when his form was very moderate for some time and he had only won three small races before he got into the Massachusetts Handicap with a featherweight and won it, in a nine-furlong record for the track, from a good horse in Foxborough, who was giving him 8 lbs more than weight-for-age. He then met the great Whirlaway, who was giving him 13 lbs. 'Mr Longtail', and I must say from his photographs I have never seen a horse with a longer one, as Whirlaway was popularly known, started at odds-on with War Relic second favourite. The Triple Crown winner trailed the field for the first half mile and then started his old bad habit of bearing out losing several lengths. He was wide on the outside when he caught War Relic right on the line. The horses were so far apart that it was impossible for onlookers to tell which had won, neither could the judge. It required an enlarged photograph for him to award the race to Whirlaway, and even then many disagreed with him although, personally, I think one could have slipped a razor blade between War Relic's nose and the line drawn on the photograph. The pair soon met again, with War Relic penalised 2 lbs, in a race run too slow for Whirlaway to get in his run, used so devastatingly against tired horses and War Relic was able to slip the field and win by four and a half lengths. War Relic never won again, so his racing fame rests solely on his two races with Whirlaway. He was no champion at stud but he sired some good horses.

As we have seen, his chestnut son, Battlefield, was bred most unusually by reason of War Relic being inbred with only two free generations (3 × 3) to both Rock Sand and Fairy Gold. The dam of Battlefield was Dark Display, who was by Fairy Gold's son, Fair Play. Thus the mare Fairy Gold made those three appearances in his fourth remove.

Buyers, without reason, often fight shy of inbreeding and Mr Widener, a chairman of the American Jockey Club, was able to pick Battlefield up for a mere $4,500. What a bargain he proved, for he was the best two-year-old of his year winning more than his fair share of the big prizes, running on strongly from sixth place in the Futurity to win going away at the end of the six and a half furlongs. His stake earnings clocked up a record for a juvenile up to that time. In his first appearance next season he ran second to Uncle Miltie, which must have pleased handicapper J. B. Campbell as he had placed the latter, against the vast majority of opinion, 2 lbs above Battlefield in the Experimental Free Handicap. Battlefield was sent back to the farm for a rest. Although he did not win a classic, Battlefield ran most consistently and in a dozen outings at three won half of his races including the Dwyer and the Travers Stakes and was second in the others including the Belmont, which might have been a little too far for him.

War Relic's son, Intent, who was to hand on the line in America, was one of the best handicap stayers of his day. He won eight races and was unplaced three times before he bowed a tendon. Among his many stakes wins were the San Juan Capistrano twice and the Santa Anita Maturity; in addition to his wins he was disqualified after winning the Santa Anita Handicap. In his very first crop he sired Intentionally.

Intentionally was one of the best four two-year-olds in a vintage year of First Landing, Tomy Lee and Restless Wind in 1958. He was out of a daughter of Discovery, so had Fair Play twice in his fourth remove. He won his first two races by four and six lengths and then led all the way to win from the previously unbeaten Easy. He then got beaten two or three times with top weight, once by Democracy by a nose. He won the Belmont Futurity by running the field off their feet, and was nearly knocked over by Tomy Lee in the Champagne Stakes finishing third but being moved up second when Tomy Lee was disqualified. After that, he coasted home in the Pimlico Futurity. The next season he appeared as a strongly muscled sprinter with big quarters. Early outings showed that a mile was his limit. He was in a lot of trouble in the Delaware Valley Stakes but came clear to win. He missed the Preakness, to take the Withers Mile. Carrying top weight and giving lumps away to all the field, he won the Warren Wright Memorial Mile. Leading all the way, he equalled the world record in, what Frank Talmadge Phelps, the American correspondent of the *Bloodstock Breeders' Review*, describes as, 'an astonishing display of pure "zip" '. At Belmont, again with top weight and again giving lumps all round, he led every step of the way and simply lost his opponents to win by ten lengths.

Intentionally's son Tentam was a most versatile performer, winning big races in sprints, handicaps and on grass. At three, getting 9 lbs more than weight-for-age, he beat Key to The Mint in the Metropolitan Handicap at Belmont. He ran third to Secretariat's stable companion, Riva Ridge, in the Brooklyn Handicap at Aqueduct. Back at Belmont, Tentam won the Governor's Handicap and was then bought by E. P. Taylor's Windfields Stud for $2,200,000, a record price for a horse in training. After winning the United Nations Handicap on grass at Atlantic City beating Star Grass by four lengths, he was then syndicated at $4,000,000 and retired to stud at Windfields Farm, where he sired Great Neck to win the 1980 International Championship in Canada.

Another son of Intentionally was Group Plan, who won the Jockey Club Gold Cup in 1975. Intentionally's son, In Reality, was out of My Dear Girl, a champion two-year-old and a granddaughter of War Relic; In Reality was thus inbred to War Relic with two free generations (3 × 3), having Fair Play three times in his fifth remove. The juvenile crop which included Intentionally's son In Reality in 1966, did not at first seem to be a top-class one like that of his sire's, although the next season revealed a vintage classic crop with a champion in Damascus and a couple of famous names in Dr Fager and Buckpasser. In Reality was among the best of three or four of his fellows at two. Next year In Reality, leading all the way, won the Hibiscus Stakes at Hialeah over seven furlongs. Then came the first of his meetings with Biller in a race confined to Florida-breds. He had to give 13 lbs to Biller and lost by half a length. In the Flamingo Stakes In Reality tried to set the pace all the way but was beaten by more than three lengths by Reflected Glory. At Gulfstream Park he met Biller again, this time the pair of them carrying the same weight, and In Reality reversed the decision by the same distance that Biller had beaten him previously; Reason to Hail was third. This last one started favourite with his stable companion, Reflected Glory, for the Florida Derby, which race appeared to be the opportunity for sorting out the local three-year-olds. Tumble Wind, an invader from California made a pretty hot pace with In Reality behind him. Two furlongs from home Tumble Wind swerved badly, causing Reason to Hail to check badly. In Reality was left clear to win by two and a half lengths from Biller, with Reason to Hail closing rapidly to miss second place by a neck.

In Reality then found Damascus too much for him in the Preakness being beaten by two and a half lengths but he was four lengths in front of the third. He then came out to meet the unbeaten Dr Fager in a field of four which was virtually a match. 'The Doctor' started favourite at 10–3 on and broke with a slight lead angling in on the first turn leaving chaos behind him. In Reality eventually sorted himself out but Dr Fager was away in front and won by six and a half lengths, with In Reality twelve lengths in front of the third. Dr Fager was disqualified and his rider suspended. In his first race against older horses In Reality won easily, as he did against his confreres the next time out. Again Damascus beat him easily, this time by seven lengths in the American Derby in a track-record's time. The next season, In Reality won the Metropolitan Mile and the even more valuable John C. Campbell Handicap; in all he won fourteen races.

In Reality has been most successful at stud. He was the leading sire of juveniles in 1977 and has been continually among the leading sires. He has replanted a classic-winning branch of the Matchem line in England. His son, Known Fact, was a bit of a problem early in his career: he was a desperate puller, very difficult to settle and, after winning his maiden, in his next two races beat himself rather than being beaten. Phil Bull tells us that both he and Willie Carson had learnt a lot about each other by the time the colt ran in the Middle Park. Taken down to the start early, Carson, when they jumped, managed to get him covered up in a small field. The Gimcrack winner, Sonnen Gold, was the first to show, then the unbeaten Snapper Point took it up and then the favourite, Lord Seymour, was sent to the front but a furlong out Known Fact sailed past Lord Seymour and held off Sonnen Gold to win by half a length. Willie Carson immediately announced that he would win the Guineas on Known Fact, but the bookmakers did not agree with him. Known Fact came out the next season to run a promising fourth in the Greenham and Carson reaffirmed his opinion. Even so he started at 14–1 for the Two Thousand Guineas, in which Nureyev started favourite. Both ridden from behind, the favourite and Known Fact passed the leaders coming into the Dip. Nureyev, hard ridden by Paquet with his whip going on his offside, tended to drift over towards Known Fact, who was on his nearside, and just hung on to pass the post first by a neck. Nureyev had caused no interference to Known Fact but his disqualification followed. Two furlongs out, Paquet, sitting back last on Nureyev, had found himself behind a wall of horses and had barged recklessly through the field. Posse, on his right, had to be snatched up and was nearly brought down. Later Posse collided with Taufan knocking this horse out of the race. Posse got out of all his trouble to finish fast and run third threequarters of a length behind Known Fact. The stewards stood Paquet down and, under the ridiculous English rule which requires the horse to suffer with its rider, placed Nureyev last instead of third behind Posse.

Known Fact did not get his full credit for his Two Thousand Guineas victory as there was something secondhand about it. He had had a clear run and Nureyev had beaten him and it seems possible that, but for the interference Posse suffered, he might have done so as well. After the race Known Fact went down with bronchitis and did not run again until August, when he finished fifth at Deauville. After that Known Fact was never beaten. His meeting with Posse was keenly looked forward to in the Waterford Crystal Mile at Goodwood, but the latter went down with a cough.

Known Fact met his rivals at worse than weight-for-age in this race. Having got him covered up, Carson had quite a job getting him through between Night Alert, who had been fourth, moved up to third in the Guineas and had since won the Prix Jean Prat, and Hard Fought, winner of the Jersey Stakes at Ascot. In the last furlong he managed to get in front to win by a neck from Hard Fought with Night Alert, who had to be snatched up in the last few yards. Lester Piggott on Night Alert objected to Hard Fought, but the objection was overruled. After that Known Fact trotted in by three lengths at Doncaster. Then came his great race with the champion four-year-old miler, Kris. They met in the Queen Elizabeth II Stakes at Ascot, a race that had been among the many of Kris's victories the previous season. In a race run at a blistering pace, Known Fact gradually got up to Kris in the last furlong to win by a neck, their nearest opponent being six lengths off. This made Known Fact the champion miler as Nureyev was not raced after the Guineas, and Known Fact had improved a lot since. Known Fact is a very good-looking medium sized black colt with a star and two hind pasterns running up white into his fetlocks. He is the first classic-winning male scion of the Matchem line to stand in England since Coronach fifty years ago. He carries a great responsibility.

Relic was the son of War Relic that revitalised the Matchem line in Europe. He was a black colt and as a two-year-old won three races and was second twice in five starts in the United States in 1947. He won the Hopeful Stakes and was second in the Saratoga Special to Better Self, the son of War Admiral's good daughter, Bee Mac. He was rated only 3 lbs behind Citation, who was acclaimed as the best horse in America since Man o'War. Relic did not meet Citation as a two-year-old nor, by bad luck, did he the next season. He won the Hibiscus Stakes over six furlongs and the seven-furlong Bahamas Handicap at Hialeah and then wrenched his back. It was hoped to get him right for the Flamingo in order to challenge Citation, but it was not to be. With Relic out of the way, Citation had no difficulty in winning by six lengths. After standing for a season at stud in America, Relic crossed to France to stand at M. Dupré's stud at Calvados with Tantieme, where he had a great deal of success.

Buisson Ardent was a chestnut colt by Relic bred by the late Aga Khan and was unbeaten as a two-year-old. His first three races were scampers over the equivalent of four and a half furlongs at Deauville. He then crossed over to Newmarket for the Middle Park Stakes. Fog grounded Alec Head, the great French trainer, and Poincelet, the French jockey, on the other side of the Channel, so Doug Smith got a chance ride. Acting on misunderstood instructions from the colt's escort, Doug Smith sent Buisson Ardent out in front all the way in the manner in which he had won his previous dashes down the Deauville course. The six furlongs at Newmarket called for more stamina, and more restraint. Coming up the hill from the Dip he was strongly challenged by Edmundo and by Final Court trying to come in between the pair. The Relic colt held on to win by a short head from Edmundo with Final Court a head away third. The following season Buisson Ardent won the French Two Thousand Guineas, in which he met another two other sons of War Relic in Polic and El Relicario. Polic had won the Prix d'Arenberg as a two-year-old and had been placed 4 lbs below him in the French Free Handicap and, the next season, won the Prix Daphnis. A pacemaker led into the straight followed by Polic, El Relicario and Buisson Ardent. The last named went ahead to win easily by two and a half lengths from El Relicario, Tenareze, Verriers and Polic all in a bunch, a short head, two necks and half a length between them. Buisson Ardent failed to stay in the Derby and then crossed over to Ascot for a magnificent race for the St James's Palace Stakes. Ratification and Pirate King were fighting a great battle when Poincelet on Buisson Ardent joined issue. Jockey Bill Rickaby found Pirate King in the enclosure for the second and Buisson Ardent in there for the third. Shaking his head he reluctantly rode Ratification into the winner's enclosure while they waited for the judge to study the photo. Pirate King first, Buisson Ardent second, Ratification third – two short heads. After two defeats in France Buisson Ardent retired to stud.

In 1959, two good colts by Relic appeared – Venture and Mincio. Venture, a full brother to Buisson Ardent, was bred by and raced for the Aly Khan. A brown colt with a blaze and four white stockings, Venture had won two races in France before crossing the Channel to contest the Imperial Produce Stakes as Venture VII. He beat a moderate field effortlessly by a length and a half. Following in his brother's footsteps he then won the Middle Park Stakes. Starting at 4–1 on, he strode away to win with a ton in hand by two lengths. Naturally, on these performances Venture VII started favourite for the Two Thousand Guineas. At the widest apart they possibly could have been on the wide Rowley Mile, Martial, on the stands rail, and Venture, on the far rails, were left in front a furlong from home with nothing able to go with them. George Moore was riding Venture, who began to loaf, for all he was worth, while Ron Hutchinson on Martial was pushing his mount out under the nose of the spectators. With either out of the way, the other was a winner by four lengths but neither jockey knew which had won until a roar from the bookmakers heralded the victory of Martial, the outsider. Incidentally, trained by Paddy Prendergast, Martial was the first Irish-trained horse to win the Two Thousand Guineas. Venture failed to stay in the Eclipse and then met his rival, Martial, in the Sussex Stakes at Goodwood. Interest in the meeting was diluted by Martial being set to give 6 lbs to Venture. It is, I suppose, heresy to draw attention to the many top-class races spoilt by ridiculous conditions, which could have been fine races and a better test of the horses concerned if left to the discretion of the handicapper. Naturally Venture was favourite and naturally Venture won with Martial second. This added nothing to the stature of Venture nor detracted from that of Martial. Venture returned to France and ran twice more; on his last appearance he finished third to Mincio.

Relic's son Mincio won twice as a two-year-old, in his last race beating the filly Marella and Pen Mane. He met Pen Mane again the next season in the French Two Thousand Guineas. Pen Mane went to the front at the entrance to the straight pursued by Mincio, who succeeded in getting up to win by a short head, although he was hanging out badly. He ran second in the Prix Lupin to Charlottesville, but failed to stay in the French Derby in which he ran ninth to the same horse. Later in the season Mincio won three races off the reel to prove himself the best horse of his generation over shorter distances.

While Mincio and Venture were performing in their classic

year, Relic had departed to England. Besides those mentioned he left behind him in France Reinata (Prix d'Arenberg), Tactic (Prix la Rochette, Prix Salamandre), Relance (Handicap Optional and Prix la Camargo), Nordic (Prix Lagrange), Blockhaus (Prix Edmond Blanc and Prix d'Ispahan), Texana (Prix des Reve d'Or and Prix d'Arenburg), Mystic (Prix des Reves d'Or), Iadwiga (Prix la Rochette and Prix Chloe), Gric (Prix Daru), Flying Relic (Prix Delartre), and O'Grady (second to Tanerko in the Prix Juigne).

Relic also got the brilliant sprinter Edellic (Prix du Gros Chene twice, Prix de l'Abbaye de Longchamp, Prix de Petit Couvert twice, Prix de Seine-et-Oise, Prix de Meutry) and the flying filly, Exanita, who won the Prix de l'Abbaye de Longchamp twice.

Pieces of Eight, trained in Ireland by Vincent O'Brien, was a black colt, a beautifully bred son of Relic out of Baby Doll by Dante out of Jack Gerber's good filly Bebe Grande by Niccolo Dell'Arca out of Grande Corniche by Panorama. Both Dante and Bebe Grande's sires are out of Nogara, to whom Baby Doll is inbred 3 × 3. The speed in his pedigree may explain why Pieces of Eight was not entered for the Derby; in any case he was slow to come to hand. Vincent O'Brien let him have his first race against top-class horses in the Eclipse in 1966. In a pretty star-studded field at Sandown it was obvious some way from home that there was only one in it. Lester Piggott, on Pieces of Eight, was standing high in his stirrups in second place as they turned into the straight. Lester then let him go and won unchallenged by two lengths from Ballyciptic, with the favourite, Pretendre, third. The race was thus one-two for Ireland. The pair returned to England from Ireland to run out first and second again in the Champion Stakes, this time it was a grimly fought battle, with Piggott at his greatest forcing Pieces of Eight back in the last few strides to regain the lead from Ballyciptic.

Pieces of Eight went to stud in Italy. After the successes in Italy of his son, Stateff, who was born in England, he returned in 1978. Stateff was a consistent runner. His most important performance was in the Italian Jockey Club Gold Cup when he beat the 10–1 on favourite, the famous New Zealand horse Balmerino, in the steward's room in October 1977. It was an odd sort of race. Three furlongs out Red Arrow was in the lead and going well when he shied at a flock of pigeons getting up in front of him. Swerving from them he hit the rails and caught a leg in an upright, which he dragged after him until he was pulled up. This left Balmerino in front far earlier than his jockey wanted and instead of being the challenger, he became the challenged. It was Stateff who challenged, and stuck desperately to the hot favourite. He got his head in front but Balmerino came again and, although he was a short head to the good passing the post, he had interfered with Stateff close home and was disqualified. Stateff's connections accepted an invitation to run in the Washington International, but unfortunately he suffered minor injuries being loaded into the truck to go to Laurel Park from New York and was withdrawn.

Thus the Matchem line in England through Relic is one of pure speed as Polic handed it on to Polyfoto winner of the Nunthorpe (now disguised under the pseudonym of the William Hill Sprint Championship to the shame of the York Race Committee). Polyfoto sired Valeriga who won two Group 3 races in England and was third in the Prix de l'Abbaye Longchamp and the filly Clear Picture in France, also winner of two Group 3 races and fourth in the French One Thousand Guineas. Polyfoto also got Bay Express, the champion sprinter in England, winner of the King's Stand Stakes and the Nunthorpe. So far Bay Express has sired three group winners – Shoot Clear over a mile, All Systems Go over a mile as a two-year-old and Appaloosa, winner of the Prix Chevalier de Steurs at Ostend.

Bibliography

The Bloodhorse
The Bloodhorse Stallion Register
The Bloodstock Breeder's Review
The British Racehorse
Daily Record
The European Racehorse
French Breeding Bulletin
New Zealand Breeder's Thoroughbred Bulletin
Pacemaker
Racing Record
Racing Update
Racehorses of – Timeform Publications
Return of Mares – Weatherbys
Sires for 19 – Pacemaker Organisation
The South African Racehorse
South African Bloodstock Breeders' Review
Sporting Life
The Stallion Book – Weatherbys
Stallion Register – Form Organisation
Statistical Record – Weatherbys
The Thoroughbred Record
The Thoroughbred Record Sire Book
The Thoroughbred Record Statistical Review

Admiral Rous and the British Turf – T. H. Bird

American Horses and Horse Breeding – Dimon
Animal Breeding – A. L. Hagedoorn
Ashgill – John Osborne
The Australian and New Zealand Thoroughbred – Ross du Bourg
Autobiography – Mark Twain
Bloodstock Breeding – Sir Charles Leicester
The Blue Ribbon of the Turf – Louis Henry Curzon
The Breeding of the Racehorse – F. Beckeer
Breeding Management – Equine Research Publications
Breeding Racehorses from Cluster Mares – Dennis Craig
Breeding Thoroughbreds – John F. Wall
Breeding to Race – Sir Rhys Llewellyn
Brigadier Gerard – John Hislop
British Bloodlines – Jerdien & Kaye
The British Thoroughbred Horse – William Allison
The Captain – Bill Curling
Chartism – Carlyle
A Classic Connection – Michael Seth-Smith
The Classic Connection – Peter Prior
The Classic Racehorse – Peter Willett
Les Croisements Rationnels – Vuillier (Lottery)
Dams of Winners – H. E. Keylock
Dams of Winners in South Africa – Jockey Club of South Africa
The Derby 1919–1947 – George Melton
Donoghue Up – Steve Donoghue
Equine Genetics and Selection Procedure – Equine Research Publications
Fair Exchange – Humphrey Finney
Focus on Racing – Norman Pegg
The Functional Development of the Thoroughbred – Franco Varola
General Stud Book – Weatherbys
Genetics and Horse Breeding – William E. Jones
Good Days – Meyrick Good
The Great Breeders and their Methods – Abram S. Hewitt
Henry Chaplin – Marchioness of Londonderry
History of the Derby Stakes – Roger Mortimer
The History of the English Turf – T. A. Cook
History of the St Leger Stakes – J. S. Fletcher

The Horse Breeder's Handbook – Joseph Osborne
Horse Breeding in Theory and Practice – B. von Oettingenz
How to Breed a Racehorse – Michael Miller
An Introduction to the Thoroughbred – Peter Willett
Just My Story – Steve Donoghue
The Life of Mat Dawson – E. M. Humphris
Makers of the Modern Thoroughbred – Peter Willett
The Mating of Thoroughbred Horses – H. E. Keylock
Memoirs of a Racing Journalist – Sidney Galtrey
Men and Horses I Have Known – George Lambton
My Lost Youth – Longfellow
My Story – Sir Gordon Richards
Names in Pedigrees – Joe Palmer
Pedigrees of Leading Winners 1912–59 – Franklin E. Birch
Pedigrees of Leading Winners 1960–80, 1981–84 – Michael
    Pickering and Martin Ross
Post Haste – Edgar Britt
Prix de l'Arc de Triomphe – Fitzgerald Seth-Smith
Racing Romance – S. Theodore Felstead
Sire Lines – Abram S. Hewitt
South African Thoroughbred Families – Edmund Nelson
Sporting Stories – Thormanby
Stud Book Lore – C. M & R. M. Prior
Stud Managers' Course, Lexington 1973
Tesio-Master of Matings – Ken Maclean
The Tesio Myth – Franco Varola
The Thoroughbred – Peter Willett
Thoroughbred Breeding of the World – Podzun Verlag
The Thoroughbred Mares' Record 1850–1928 – J. F. Mainwaring
    Sharp
A Treatise on Thoroughbred Selection – Donald Lesh
Turf Memories of Sixty Years – Alexander Scott
Typology of the Racehorse – Franco Varola
Winners of Major Races from 1900 – Peter Pring

APPENDIX 1
THE MATCHEM LINE

Sham (The Godolphin Arabian) – Roxana by Bald Galloway
Cade 1734 – Mare by Partner

Matchem 1748 – Mare by Snap

Conductor 1767 – Brunette by Squirrel
Trumpator 1782 – Young Giantess by Diomed
Sorcerer 1796 – Houshton Lass by Sir Peter
Comus 1809 – Clinkerina by Clinker
Humphrey Clinker 1822 – Mare by Cervantes
Melbourne 1834 – Mowerina by Touchstone
West Australian 1850 – Mare by Birdcatcher (*see also p. 140*)
Solon 1861 – Ballyroe by Belladrum
Barcaldine 1878 – Novitiate by Hermit
Marco 1892 – Lady Villikins by Le Var
Marcovil 1903 – Toute Suite by Sainfoin
Hurry On 1913 – Double Life by Bachelor's Double
Precipitation 1933 – Noorani by Nearco – Empire Glory
Sheshoon 1956

AMERICAN BRANCH

West Australian 1850 – Emilia by Young Emilius
Australian 1857 – Aerolite by Lexington
Spendthrift 1876 – Cinderella by Blair Athol
Hastings 1893 – Fairy Gold by Bend Or
Fair Play 1905 – Mahubah by Rock Sand
Man O'War 1917 – Friar Carse by Friar Rock
War Relic 1938 – Liz F by Bubbling Over
Intent 1948 – My Recipe by Discovery – **Relic** 1945
Intentionally 1956 – My Dear Girl by Rough n'Tumble
In Reality 1964 – Tamarett by Tim Tam
Known Fact (USA) 1977

Relic 1945 – Polaire II by Le Volcan
Polic 1953 – Brabantia by Homeyway
Polyfoto 1962 – Pal Sinna by Palestine
Bay Express 1971

Relic – Djenne by Djebel
Olden Times 1958 – Dearest Mommy by Summer Tan
Full Pocket 1969

INDEX

Chetwynd, George, 26, 31, 52, 54, 63, 80
Chifney, Will, 20-1
Childeric, 49
Childs, Joe, 103, 105, 107
Cicero, 81, 115
Ciel Etoile, 108
Citation, 131
Clarence, 112
Clark, Sterling, 51, 123
Clear Picture, 135
Clemence, 24
Cliveden Stud, 116
Cloister, 87
Cloncarrig, 95
Coaraze, 108
Coastal Guard, 40
Coin of the Realm, 114
Coke, Edward, 2-3, 5
Colin, 55, 56
Collaborator, 101
Colorado, 105-7, 117
Colours (of horses), 107
Comedienne, 109
Comus, 31, 34
Concertina, 67
Conductor, 11
Constable (jockey), 48-9
Cool Customer, 96-7
Coronach, 45, 104-7, 117, 131
Coronach's sons, 108-9
Coronaise, 107
Coronation V, 18
Corrida, 107-8
Corrie Roy, 54
Cotherstone, 14
Cottage, 87, 94-6
Cottage Rake, 96-7
County Fermoy, 94
Craganour, 76-9
Craig Eleyr, 67
Cranach, 108
Craneur, 108
Cresta Run, 115
Cripple, 7
Cromwell, 95
Crown Prince, 91
Crusader, 61, 120
Curzon, 79

Curzon, Frank, 110-11
Custance, Henry, 23, 36, 43, 47
Cyllene, 32

Daily Mail, 111
Daily Telegraph, 65
Dalby, 38
Damascus, 128-9
Dan Sparling, 54
Dante, 118
Darius, 123
Dark Display, 124, 127
Dark Legend, 86
Dark Star, 57
Darley Arabian, 4, 10
Darling's Dam, 70
Darling, Fred, 76, 100-1, 104
Davy Jones, 90-1, 95
Dawson, Mat, 23, 40, 47
Day Comet, 75-6
Day, Alfred, 22-3
Day, William, 22-3, 32, 54
Deception, 27
Defence, 13
Democracy, 127
Derby 1913, 74-6
Derby, Lord, 46, 100, 110, 121
Desert Chief, 89
Desmond, 79
Deux Pour Cent, 113
Devon Loch, 91, 95
Diligence, 111-13
Dines, Johnny, 76
Diomed, 9, 50
Diomedes, 92
Discovery, 57-8, 117, 127
Display, 56, 61, 124
Doctor Syntax, 14-15, 17, 31
Don Fulano, 51
Donoghue, Steve, 15, 63-4, 67-9, 76, 84-6, 101-2, 106, 111
Dr Frager, 128-9
Duchess, 10
Durham, Lord, 75, 83, 117

Early Mist, 98
Easter Hero, 88-90, 92-3
Easy, 127